shadows

For Sarah

Tenderly

at City Lights

Xam

June 2008

King of Shadows

Aaron Shurin

City Lights Books
San Francisco

Cover design: Stefan Gutermuth / double-u-gee
Text design and composition: Gambrinus

Editor: Robert Sharrard

Library of Congress Cataloging-in-Publication Data

Shurin, Aaron, 1947
  King of shadows / Aaron Shurin
      p. cm.

ISBN 978-0-87286-490-0
1. Shurin, Aaron, 1947– 2. Poets, American—United States—Biography. 3. Gay authors—United States—Biography. 4. Gay authors—
California—San Francisco—Biography. 5. Gay men—California—San
Francisco—Biography. I. Title. II. Series

               PS3569.H86Z46 2006
               811' 54—dc22

                       2007052478

City Lights Books are published at the City Lights Bookstore,
261 Columbus Avenue, San Francisco, CA 94133

www.citylights.com

Thanks to the following journals and anthologies, in which some of this work first appeared: *26; Absomaly; Five Fingers Review; Lodestar Quarterly; Love, Castro Street; New American Writing; The New Review of Literature; Onedit; Robert Duncan and Denise Levertov: The Poetry of Politics, the Politics of Poetry; Switchback; Talisman; Tolling Elves; Traverse; Volt;* and *zyzzyva.*

⊡　⊡　⊡

I would also like to thank a number of friends and colleagues who gave careful consideration to this book in whole or in part, among them Kate Brady, Lewis Buzbee, Norma Cole, Thomas Evans, Susan Friedland, Bob Glück, James Hass, Rob Kaufman, Silvana Nova, Michael Palmer, Rosita Perrino, Jocelyn Saidenberg, Craig Seligman, Tavi Storer, and Susan Thompson, as well as many generously attentive students at the University of San Francisco. Special acknowledgement is due to the California Arts Council, the San Francisco Arts Commission, and the Fund for Poetry for heartening support.

CONTENTS

THE SHRINE

Birds are scary as shit, it's as simple as that. Of *course* they're dinosaurs—you can see the predatory forward lean, feel the grip of the scuttling clawed legs. Virginia Woolf knew this exactly; her thunder-footed robins have bayonets for beaks as they pierce "the soft, monstrous body of the defenseless worm." Literary critics like to see these stabbing pistons as stand-ins for the penis, but to me Woolf's fear of birds is a primary shrivel predating her phallophobia. In the end, it was birds talking Greek outside the window that sent her over the maddened edge.

Some animals take projection kindly (*Here, poochie!*) but the winged race is ruthless in resisting anthropomorphism. They strut and strike and take to the air with contemptuous subjectivity. If I say I admire hawks inordinately, it's because the root of awe is terror: Their uncompromising elegance, their brutal finesse, make me feel like a squirmy thing at the bottom of a food chain.

I'm afraid of birds; I adore dogs, those lollipops; and I'm allergically disinterested in cats. As for fish, who could be anything but neutral? And yet, this is a story about fish. Like all fish tales it grows larger in the telling.

It gains impetus from the '60s so psychedelia upholds it, colors it like scales of a trout, emblem of an era saturated in scintillating transformation and quicksilver shifts in point of view.

⊞   ⊞   ⊞

We had stepped out of our Berkeley-student brown-shingled house in 1966, and as soon as the door had opened it was clear that LSD had opened a door. Instantly, across the street, the fir tree—the *first* tree—the *echt* tree—called for a new organic geometry; the first lesson, the *echt* lesson: that rooted plants were really streaming lines of energy, crosshatched but constantly moving, so that matter had a grid but didn't settle, as if a breeze blew particles into temporary shape, flexible current of form. If trees are visible, electromagnetic shifting shapes then what are we? Mark hallucinated an endless hulk of shame, accusatory and paralyzing; Roger felt a sensual light that loosened his body from its good-guy practice; Roosevelt locked on looming monsters drawing near and couldn't keep looking. I, who already fed on gay shame, exploding sex, and the demons of self criticism, saw instead (this was pharmaceutical Sandoz acid straight out of Switzerland) my literal brain in its pure materiality, a house-sized red mucosa of corridors and tunnels through which I actually walked, craning my neck, ducking and gaping. Like a museum tour guide, I could read the shadowy walls of my intents and operations, dispassionate.

This fixed locus of elemental pulp was related to the tree's flowing electric whiz, but I knew it was also the means by which tree, branch, and root were apprehended. Pulsating mechanism: I could sense the envisioning apparatus, was ready to grasp the means of focus, lens, and imprint—when Roosevelt's incoming monsters proved too much for him to handle, and his cries drew me zooming back to help.

If I say that in the end I put the active tree back in its street-bound plot, the brain back in its bony temple, and walked on, I'm merely suggesting that some hours later the drug wore off. I still can't tell you whether the village violinist who sat alone on top of a table at 4 A.M. in a closed but spotlighted Telegraph Avenue coffee house was factually there. In 1966 one accommodated hallucination or psychic blur on principle and faith, as indicators of various social forces weakening or growing strong, collective markers all of excited threshold, border, liminal edge.

▣   ▣   ▣

The following year I was back in L.A., home for vacation in the wake of San Francisco's epochal Summer of Love, where I'd dutifully purchased a set of beads to adorn my student's corduroy jacket—circle around a square—and had listened, stoned, to Ginsberg and Leary exhort at the Human Be-In in Golden Gate Park. My Jewish hair was beginning to take on its natural sausage curls, the same ones my mother battled with a permafrost of hair spray and bleach. By now the hair had commandeered my ears and was threatening my shoulders; a mustache tickled my upper lip and the men who kissed it. It was still several years before the invention of my parents' own mantra, summarizing my brother and me and our endless "fresh" ways—gay, radical, outspoken—in a tidy analysis reduced to the mournfully repeated phrase, "*Berkeley ruined you!*"

But I've been trying to tell you about the fish. I circle around the moment like ripples on a pond, to find its point of impact, progenitor of successive waves of cause and effect, heart of a matrix. I circle because though contemporary events have mere synchronicity, the past, I know, is always interconnected. We live out the enmeshed through-lines, but the connections are revealed only when read backwards. Slowly I push and part, circuit and loop; memory itself is dark water through which I swim thickly. I can just see a twinkling light above the surface, origin of an anecdote that swells in its telling, so I move as the current moves and the story sways.

Mantras were definitely in the air, and the idea of meditation, if not the practice, had already caught my eager, wandering attention. In those days you could drive at a leisurely pace through westward L.A. canyons and hills, where Pacific Palisades crested peacefully over the still-blue ocean. There on the left, before the winding road drove down to breakers, caught in the glistening western light, was a Hollywood mirage of minarets and cupolas—a quiet path circuiting a quiet lake—known as the Paramahansa Yogananda Self-Realization Fellowship and Church of All Religions. Oasis and succor for smog-weary Angelenos, it caused me numerous times to put on the brakes, and finally I postponed a swim to get closer to the shrine's Taj Mahal–ish pergolas. Had I read, at that point, Yogananda's famous *Autobiography of a Yogi*? I'm not sure, though I can still see the rust-colored cover featuring a photo of Yogananda's bland, puffy face, with his long wavy hair worthy of a maenad.

The kind meditative lake cleared out the L.A. fracas; I took a stroll along the periphery where afternoon sun stripped back the surface of the water and let one look *through*. "I'll be a world-famous American yogi," I thought to myself. "Without drugs I'll pierce the Maya, and understand the illusory nature of all material things." I shook a pebble from my rubber flip-flop. "I'll levitate, free myself from gay shame, have blond surfer-like acolytes, and live comfortably in a cave in India."

I *could* be more generous: I'm sure I also thought about stopping the Vietnam War, detonating the nuclear family, and freeing all political prisoners. I would have imagined all of this as simultaneously possible—delusional grandeur as well as righteous moral imperative—because I was young enough to believe unerringly in my self-realization (appropriately sited!). Later on, of course, I came to understand the crimping complexities of doubt, with that tight cap we like to call "adulthood."

The air was fresh on the ocean breeze as I stopped at a bend in the path, pond's contour and mind's pause. Crouching, I ran my hand through pebbles, idly tossed one into the lake. Plink. Ripples. I tossed another one: plink. Intersecting ripples. A great yogi breathes the tides. He knows that trees stream in immaterial currents; he maintains detachment even in Los Angeles; plink. Little fish skittered in the shallows, the water transparent around their glittery quickness. They moved together like one mind, one muscle. As I threw another pebble—as it hit the water—they constellated around it in a flash: food! Instantaneously they radiated toward the impact point, head first, ready to gulp. I was dazzled by the organization of their split-second dash; threw stone after stone, a god among fishes, toying with their instinctual, unconsidered reflexes. Little fish are squirmy things at the bottom of the food chain. Plink.

Not much better at pitching pebbles than I was at pitching a baseball, I tossed again but the small stone stuck to my fingers. Though my arm pretended to throw, no stone fell. In a second the minnows congealed toward an imaginary trajectory on the surface of the water where nothing plinked.

I did a double take, then stopped cold like a fish caught in the headlights. I thought about what I thought I saw. Carefully, deliberately, pinching only air between my fingers, I threw another non-rock. The fish sprang to action on the beam.

I looked around in something like panic. My eyes bulged; my gills gasped; I sucked uncomfortably for air. Every stable point of reference I had began to tip. What kind of mutual gaze was operating here? Suddenly I was upended by a tsunami in which all sentient beings were busy laughing: The little, unimportant, easily fooled fish had been watching *me!* Not the impact of the pebble as it fell, not the ripples on the pond, not some vague shadow moving. They were peering *through* the water *across* the inviolable surface up *into* the human air directly at me. Watching my arm, my itchy fingers. Tuned specifically to the arc of my self-infatuated game.

Alone but surrounded, I burbled like a drowning man—then shook my head and started to chuckle. No universe I'd as yet constructed admitted of such complex cross-observation. Subject voices sprang to

life around me in a newly animated interspecies pop-
ulace—and the reverberating sound spread outward in
concentric circles.

I sat for a long time at that bend in the pond while
the minnows, finished with me, went on about their
other professorial duties. This is, as I said, one of those
fish tales that lengthens in the telling, but the longer it
grows the less it deviates from the truth. An itinerary of
transformative events—mind-bending pot, LSD, psilo-
cybin; angry marches, teargassing, sit-ins; gay bars of
perdition, love balm, maddening pride; pitiless
encounter groups, visionary communes, gender
redress—swam in the lead and the wake of the flashing
sharp-eyed fish.

I watched the sparkle under the water's edge as it
retreated. I'd been humiliated beyond recognition, as
befits a very young yogi, but possibly reinvented. I
couldn't afford to take for granted purpose or position
on this axis. Standing up, I raised my eyes to painted
columns graceful in twilight. I swore to the Self-Realization Fellowship Church of All Religions that I would
change fast—and history saw to it that I did.

I recently took a house for the summer, where a garden front and back bloomed generously, incessantly, demanding unexpected attention since I'd been instructed to water only once a week, and carefully shown the system of soaker hoses and split faucets that promised one long morning's relaxed consideration. On the fifth sunny day, when the nasturtium beds and Hawaiian firecrackers didn't so much wilt as *melt*— their shriveling had a pendulous, amorphous droop to it, Dali-esque; the crisp, colorful, cellular flags had turned into something like gummy puddles—I snapped myself together, countermanded the instructional rule, and started watering by hand to save the jungle from extinction.

"I've just been here since January, " the occupant had told me over the phone when we started to work out the terms of my sublet. "I've done a ton of weeding for you," she added right before my arrival, "and I worked all weekend spreading bags of cocoa-shell mulch, so you won't have to do much. Just water once a week." She wasn't lying; she just hadn't yet spent a summer in the house and was innocently unaware of the bone-white

July sun that bore down on this part of Marin county with unremitting Aegean ferocity—and so was also unprepared for the failure of her delicate soaking system that needed unrestricted at-home time and spring-like regularly moist soil.

It took three weeks for the yellow nasturtiums to re-inscribe themselves into paragraphs, but I'd managed to quickly save all of the rest, and day by day the garden grew fuller, taller, thicker, more populated. The cocoa mulch held the weeds back brilliantly, and offered the bonus of wafting the scent of chocolate into the house each time I opened the front or back door. New perennials constantly sprang up unannounced, filling in small barren spots with their surprise attractions: tiny yellow-chinned violets, effulgent purple dahlias, a two-headed pink gerbera daisy, willful strands of magenta sweet peas that would climb your hand if you left it resting too long, one pure but incongruous fumy gardenia—while over the course of the summer the stalwart artichoke opened its crustacean leaves into a livid, heaving crown of scintillating blue, enrapturing the bees who grazed *inside* the oversized bloom as if it were a meadow; the strawberries dropped their hot, sweet hearts into my hands by the cupful; and the morning glories, who *owned* the house, raged over the front wall, withered in a morning minute, and bled their indigo trumpets into translucent pink disks, shedding them finally like wrinkled carapaces onto the porch steps—then blared moonily again the next day, blue-bright as high twilight and uncountable in their florescent profusion. Oregano and marjoram blossomed and began to dry in the air, spiking the night with hot summer undertones.

Oh, I could name each flower I tended in a rapture of taxonomy and parental devotion, even though I grumbled about the unanticipated hours spent watering—the almost umbilical tether of care that shortened my freedom—and nursed a petulant feeling of having been misled about the work involved. I prodded and petted the blooms, cut back the overgrowth, pruned the spent heads and podding vines. I watered by hand, by spigot section, by soaker hose, by can, by pitcher, and by glass. I sat on the back deck facing the most abundant plot and read for hours, lifting my eyes to watch the bumblebees weigh down the lavender spears, or turn themselves over to suck in mid-air the inverted stars of the borage. I lost my way in book after book, as the pages filled with pollen, petals, glinting hummingbirds, slow leggy wasps, and honeysuckle tongues.

Each day found me more careful, more proprietary, more *taken.* And the more I tended, the more flowers came up, the rounder the grapes swelled, the higher the hollyhock grew—twelve feet, fifteen feet?—until the great angel's trumpet in one day knocked out forty colossal yellow succubi that commandeered the left side of the backyard almost howling, while on the right a massive bush of climbing roses, which had been cut back before I arrived, began to open by the dozen, dense, ruffled circlets of deep tangerine that matured into glowing apricot love-nests, seductively subtle and flamboyant at the same time, before finally releasing themselves into exhausted, overblown white. By then it was clear the garden was performing *for* me. It responded to my dutiful and generous care with creative intent—it *grew*!—and if I refrain from adding "joyously" so as not to (over) anthropomorphize, I can still insist the mutual give and take was relational. Having saved it from meltdown, brought it back to life, cultivated it, savored it, stroked it, fed it, worried over it, been endlessly startled by it and euphorically entertained, I'd clearly forged a deep reciprocal bond.

Dizzy white butterflies jagged in the evening air as I considered my complex circumstance: the affectionate fullness and the worried supervision. I tested this emotional tether as if I could see filaments straining. Bent protectively over a smiling spray of tiny violas that sprouted through cracks in the flagstone, I realized that tending the garden was just like having a new pet. I was now party to a multi-layered melding of ownership pride, tender intimacies, stern behavioral modulation, ecstatic paranormal communication, mutually generative companionship, interlocked performance and audience appreciation, even sublimated desire. (I could have *rolled* in those apricot roses—if not for the thorns.) In short, I cared for, and was beautifully taken care of.

Back in the city as August progresses I sit in my high-ceilinged, top-floor rooms, seemingly suspended among the tall elms and flowing eucalyptus in the park out front, so I'm not *without.* I have orchids to baby or mother or father, that show their appreciation extravagantly—perhaps too much so, since I only water a little and feed less—but whose showy, alien sense of color and form speak irrefutably of autonomy—and you have to maintain a certain distance with creatures from other planets. I do have burgundy gladioli in one vase, and fat, fearless sunflowers in another, but they're provisional. I read books right through from beginning to end. The fog's finally blown in on late summer winds. "If August passes/ flowerless,/ and the frosts come," writes Denise Levertov in her poem "Annuals," having tended a yearly garden that sprouted up but didn't bloom, "will I have learned to rejoice enough/ in the sober wonder of/ green healthy leaves?"

"Fine," I sigh soberly, "but what, then, will have learned to rejoice in me?" And flex my watering hand involuntarily, trying not to linger on the image of slick green grapes ready for plucking, pink roses puffing their breasts in the rousing heat and almost spraying scent, hydrangeas shading from mauve to blue in the midafternoon, ardent tendrils of morning glory twining, twining . . .

ALONG THE WAY

I walk to work through a narrow park. Traffic streams on either side while the wind runs through the grassy spaces, stirring a few fallen leaves and lifting the weight from the sun. A dozen configurations of family use the children's playground, kids on the swings and climbing contraptions, parents arrayed on benches along the periphery, watchful. The site—a large sandbox, really—has been cleared of its used needles for several years and consequently revitalized, but if the children are oblivious to history the parents maintain a tense, sober regard. I have the feeling they're observing the surroundings more than the kids, harried by tales of abductions, and it makes me feel suspect—even guilty—when I stop at a bench to look at them. The elm trees are fluffing out a few light green leaves; the eucalyptus wiggles its pendulous strips; the tall cypress preserves a natural gloom stuffed in its thick upper branches that block the sun. Why do I have to saddle the tightly clustered boughs with the word "gloom," and how does it serve me to project this emotional tenor into their innocent shade? An abandoned packet of lube—or is it glitter glue?—sparkles on the bench beside me. One transient cloud erases warmth. Mystery is the failure of description, the object's leverage on the subject. A kid slides, but there's too much friction and he has to inchworm down the last five feet. I could sleep in the sun, I could sleep any time anywhere like a stork on one leg, but this tiredness is a thought not a physical disposition. I go to work, pretending to have reached a point of comprehension while the wind picks up, quickening the clouds and raising my forelock like a handle.

◧   ◧   ◧

I get ready to walk to work again—it's my usual m.o.—on a foggy afternoon in June—no, wait, it's sunny—no, it's foggy—now it's both, will my brand-new short-sleeve shirt be warm enough after all? I pace my apartment in preparation, alternately reading, eating, checking email, as I project myself along the path I'll be taking, to the gym I might stop at first, among my colleagues with whom I'll discuss school business and then go out to dinner where I've thought about what I might eat by conjuring meals I've had there in the past: A grilled prosciutto-wrapped fig appetizer is particularly memorable. My bedroom pulsates like a jellyfish: It seems to swell, then shrink, as the sun comes out or fades. What will I be thinking of when I'm actually walking, will I think about being at home?

Here's what I do when I'm going to get a burrito: Along the way I think about what I'll order, and then say to myself, "I'd like a carnitas burrito with avocado, please," or, "a molé taco, no chips, please," in a perfect gentlemanly tone, precise and affable. I rehearse this like a mantra as I'm walking or even driving. Do I think I'll forget what I want to eat, or do I think the counter people won't understand me? Are my desires so translated through language that they need to be solidified by my preparatory order first, so that my mind is ready to be fulfilled before my stomach is? I catch myself pre-ordering this way all the time—"a morning bun to go, please"—as if my hunger weren't real until I find the words that will assuage it. By the time I'm at the counter I pronounce my phrases with a confident, improvisational air, natural and assured.

For years as I was doing things—especially when I was walking—I would narrate the unfolding events to myself in the past tense *as* they were happening. For example, if I was ambling down Market Street and saw a streetcar accident I would say to myself, "I was walking down Market Street and saw an accident." Or I would go to the produce market to buy some perfect May cherries and think, just as I was fingering the darkest and firmest, "I bought the most beautiful cherries, today." The temporal disjunction was purely literary, an urge toward framing via narration so strong that the past

felt more solid than the present—it *proved* the present—
superimposing onto mere stimuli the aura of fact. And
the kinesthetic passage of time through walking lent to
events a corporeal density that let them be fixed.

In the street on the way to the gym I pick a fight with
one of my co-workers, which is to say I mentally
embroider an argument we had yesterday by shaping my
points and leveling a few new counter-charges. My new
argument is inescapable, and victory is complete. The
sky has opened all the way from the ocean to the Bay,
with just a few wispy stragglers out of the West. It's the
last week before summer vacation so every sunny day is
an augury. The wind flaps my jacket giving me needed
underarm air. Strolling makes thought shapely. The red
bottlebrush spikes are tipped in gold; the beds of impa-
tiens mutate pink into purple. In the fresh air of my
impending vacation I find a reason to forgo the gym and
scour the streets and university grounds like a periscope.
The wind's a little wilder, now, and I'd be willing to ride
on it. Lazily I think of George Herbert's "I reade, and
sigh, and wish I were a tree." It's as if the ethereal body
suddenly desired preeminence, and you could dissolve
happily into air with your consciousness intact, being
yourself and seeing the things you see but weightlessly
navigating, at once presence and dispersal. The English
poets seem to know everything about the empire of air:
Coleridge's "Where the breeze warbles, and the mute

still air/ Is Music slumbering on her instrument," or Shelley's windward "Driving sweet buds like flocks to feed in air." The day seems grander, more promising, for my having quoted poetry. A bit lightheaded now— filled with air I might say—I arrive at work exhilarated and slightly exhausted, as if I've traveled a long distance, with numerous connections, and made it home safely with plenty of time to spare.

⊞   ⊞   ⊞

In Marin county for a summer break, I take a walk around Phoenix Lake. Nested in golden watershed hills; bordered by sinuous black oaks, bay laurel, madrones; dotted with a few hikers and a few more joggers—it gives the feeling of wild sanctuary while maintaining the man-made solace of urban proximity: It's just a reservoir. The surrounding hills swoop up in the back of each vista, alternately bronzed and barren or thickly forested. In such a protected circle the air seems to float on the air. Most other people are walking in the opposite direc- tion—I'm going counter-clockwise—and most nod hello, with a touch of suburban privilege acknowledg- ing the safety of common strangers. My gray hair helps me appear benign. I notice that I've begun to narrate my walk again, a *fait accompli* even as I begin, so that by the time I circuit a quarter of the lake I'm possessed by a feeling of deep déjà vu—as if I'd taken this entirely new excursion before—having told myself the story of its completed adventure at the outset. Soliloquy predates dialogue. The stentorian diction in *Beowulf* makes you feel as if events are being announced rather than read, a declamation instead of a narration. One mysterious bird clackety-clacks high up in the woods. A posted sign says a black bear's been spotted recently in the area; another warns of indigenous mountain lions, with details on how to react. Along the edge of the lake, passing some bicyclists, I fight off the bear in the proper way, backing slowly while raising my flapping arms and making noises; the mountain lion is more determined but my informed, if outraged, spunkiness wins the day. On a very narrow, uneven part of the path a jogging man approaches—why do people run over this uneven, root-ridged, terrain; don't they trip and doesn't it hurt their feet?—and offers me a fragile smile as I stand aside to let him pass. His female companion avoids my eyes with a grimly determined forward gaze, so I begin a theory about gender and social space, women and danger. When another running couple comes into view she nods generously while he blindly soldiers on, deconstructing my gender theory and leaving me face to face with a solitary walker. I establish a new principle about couples and single people. He's dressed like a weekend warrior in printed shorts and a floral shirt, overfilling both and moving slowly. I prepare a small greeting—is it appropriate to say something out loud, or just smile?—but he looks straight ahead without any acknowledgment. The other side of the lake appears grander at every turn because you can *see* the vista, as opposed to being *in* it—at once elevating your spirit and making you restless. I'd met an attractive young man who worked in a bookstore and with whom I discussed a new translation of *Beowulf,* directing my responses to him and then to his co-worker so as not to appear too forward—was he even gay?—or too obsessive, since I couldn't tell his age and it might have been much too young for me. His mind seemed bright, he had a gleeful, bright responsiveness, his smile was bright above his trim torso. Later, approaching the bookstore on the lookout for him, I passed a plate glass window where my instant reflection showed a rather tentative older man with silver hair, nothing at all like the charismatic person who'd been flirting with the clerk. I pluck a bay leaf, crumple it and sniff: Its menthol pierces the front lobe of your brain like a tiny needle, but it's a good pain because it gives you a tactile experience in a part of the body where you usually have only mental ones. The shadow of a turkey vulture across the path alerts me to the flight of a turkey vulture overhead: one continuous soaring arc. I have a sense of inscribing the open sky with my body, curving languorously and making big

loops of meaning above the treetops. I sit on a weathered wooden bench, take out a small Chinese notebook,
untwist my purple French ballpoint, holding it above
the paper while the wind whips off the water, too strong
to make sitting here viable for long, then write, so as not
to forget, "I wrap myself in the arms of sentences." On
the way out, I pick up the pace at a bend in the path to
better see the profile of a man walking in front of me.
Warmth still hangs in the late afternoon air like a scent,
something separate and particulate that can be dis-
persed. He carries a strange thin backpack, which I
think holds drawing implements, since he's clutching a
large sketch pad, by which, I believe, he has wrapped
himself in the arms of images. My bright blue car shines
resolutely in sunlight. As I open the door to get, in a
woman next to me opens hers to get out, sneaking a
look at me across the door frame before I drive off. The
sketcher is walking on the dusty access road in front of
me. I give him an image of pure, blue momentum as I
drive on.

GEOMANCY

On the way to the airport alone in the very stretch limo, which had turned out to be the hotel's version of a door-to-door shuttle, I scan the houses, loping roads, long slow horizon, the open bowl of the all-visible sky, and say the name "Chicago" with a shiver of pleasure, as if the actual city lay *there* in its announcement—which is true insofar as before this week I'd never been to Chicago, had only this verbal gesture, an echo of the architecture of a song I can't remember the words to, though I try to sing it a little to myself in the car, and can't exactly remember the melody either: It segues into "San Francisco" as if Judy Garland were doing a medley, while the Pakistani limo driver quizzes me about my impressions of the city, seeming particularly interested in delivering his own contradictory responses.

The downtown is handsome, carefully made, with a buoyant spaciousness unlike any other city I've seen, I tell him, and he agrees, but there's a mournfulness in his voice as his running description passes beyond the city limits, and a near-hysteria I detect in the torque of his ache as he complains, "It's all flat, ugly, so flat. You go for miles—ugly flat country, flat, flat. To find the beautiful

31

place"—he shakes his head—"you have to drive *six* hours! All flat, flat."

I look at the far views from each side of the limo to register the flatness he moans of, and it's true you can see as far as you can see in every direction: from the slight lift of the highway the sleek horizon is unpimpled by structures or trees; the sky is voluminous, noisy with clouds, an undiminished hemisphere. Gazing, I mouth to myself the other captured word that Kate used yesterday: 'prairie.' 'The Prairie.' I visualize miles of whispering grasses, acres of pure direction.

"What's the difference between The Great Plains and The Prairie?" I'd asked; neither of us was really sure. I told Kate about my one trip to Kansas City a few years back, when Richard had taken me to a scenic bluff overlooking the Missouri river. Behind the cliff top was an undulant Kansas City, MO, neighborhood, and just back of that were pleasant, rolling, tree-filled districts Richard had driven me through; in front of us, westward, was a sheer drop to the river, and then a stretching, perfectly flat plateau, with Kansas City, KS, just in the distance, a hat on a rug. I'd thought to myself, "Now begins the Great Plains. I'm literally standing with my back to the Midwest, but from my feet on out it's the Great Plains right to the Rockies!"

I slept through geography so I can't vouch for the accuracy of my coordinates, but I do know the Great

Plains lived in my speaking as if my mind had been suddenly unfettered, loosed from an unknown band, and I flooded west spreading till I couldn't see a way to stop, as far as my floating eyes could carry me, balanced as I was on the literal pitch of the vast continent's inner lip.

I take with me back to San Francisco this new matching set, two palpable phrases ready to burst—The Great Plains, The Prairie—with a feeling I can shut and open these magic boxes at will, and scoot myself out of my apartment walls in lonely emergency, to breathe-in the curative powers of space and scale. "O flots abracadabrantesques," Rimbaud addresses the ocean he's conjured, "Prenez mon cœur, qu'il soit lavé!" "O abracadabric waves, take my heart and wash it clean."

The sea unfolds.

KING OF SHADOWS

Here is the slipper, the dancing shoe as in so many other tales, a thin black casing with abrasive sole to enable the leap but stop the slide: a ballet slipper. Here is a little, charged icon, in which and through which trajectories animate and fuse, so that a foot stepping into the shoe and saying "I do" goes where the slipper goes, as if this small gesture of intention were, in fact, a magical act. A foot in a slipper takes a step: the House of Poetry, the House of Sex open their doors; night's swift dragons now purple with love's wound.

▫   ▫   ▫

In the spring of 1965, at the age of seventeen, my torso thin and sprightly, my ears elfin, I threw myself across the hallway floor of our Spanish stucco house, gesturing methodically and casting my face into a far-seeing gaze.

"I know a bank where the wild thyme blows," I intoned, vowels round and oracular—though certainly at that point I'd never seen wild thyme, as I have many times since on the summer hills of Crete, where the crushed scent underfoot freshens the hot, heavy air. I lengthened my body and balanced stiffly as though draped along rocks, hand raised to carve sonorities out of the L.A. smog.

"<u>Where oxlips and the nodding violet grows quite overcanopied with luscious woodbine</u>." Looking down at me from their stations by the bedroom door, my mother and brother absorbed this oratory impassively, audience and judge. I was a noble spirit, drunk on poetic evocation—but where had I learned such hammy declamation and Victorian poses? I'd gathered what I could from classic highbrow TV productions like "Omnibus" and "Hallmark Hall of Fame," where London superstars of the pre- and postwar eras failed to modulate their passions for the flat cathode box, but in which the gloss of high culture with its salutary purpose was permitted to flicker in gray and black across America's drowsy eyelids. Poetic diction and super-elocution were already part of my personal style, nurtured by familial continental drift, and a young life spent memorizing narrative ballads—hanging in suspense of the unfolding rhyme—and performing on stage where I was the default MC for endless talent shows, since I looked good in a bright blue suit and my extreme diction translated to the balcony. A sissy sensibility gave nuance to my bearing, making me acceptable to all parents, who misperceived me enthusiastically as "a little gentleman."

Now the high school play had been announced: *A*

Midsummer Night's Dream. I could be, I *would* be, Oberon, King of the Fairies, whose famous rhapsody on Titania's resting place would be my tryout piece. Shifting uncomfortably, I lifted my elbow, which was getting carpet burn, and pointed extravagantly to the faraway bank, replete with "<u>sweet musk roses and with eglantine</u>."

"Why are you talking like that?" my mother complained.

"What do you mean?"

Mom and Isak glanced at each other and in unison chanted, "I knooow a bank where the wiiild thyyyme bloooows," in poisonous English accents, stagy and grandiloquent.

"It's poetry!"

They chortled together, telescoping their arms out with awkward solemn purpose, and shook their heads, unconvinced. The dumb show solidified their conviction, but they *weren't* philistines so the argument wasn't about literature. They just weren't buying my freighted manner. I closed my imaginary cape in a huff and sulked into the bedroom.

The boy there under covers licked his wounds and guarded this vision of language in flower, powered by Shakespeare's nominative urge: thyme, oxlips, violets, woodbine. The closed bedroom door admitted only this floral torch that named things and lit them <u>to lead him through the glimmering night</u>.

The boy there turned in his bed, restless, a King of

Fairies but surrounded by the shadows of men, boys, men, their shadowy parts, turning in his bed, whispering, "Hey . . . Boy . . . it *can* be done; <u>pursue it with the soul of love</u>;" shadowy parts rubbing him <u>through the glimmering night</u>.

▣   ▣   ▣

The unremarkable bedroom in the unremarkable house in a remarkable wealthy colony where we were pretenders; the bedcovers brown, the bed and curtains brown. Nothing in it appeared to be mine, though the *room* was mine. Where were my things, my markings? I remember just one poor pastel (my mother an accomplished artist) that I'd copied from an old book, an ancient pious Jew with long white beard and hair, holding the sacred text in a tiny, withered, misshapen hand whose demand for complex perspective far exceeded my abilities.

Looking back I see nothing else by which I owned the space, astounding given my adult predilection for particularizing domesticity down to the floorboards. No baseball pennants—obviously!—no posters (which would decorate my dormitory walls within a year), the model planes and trains long ago sequestered. I was *off* the walls and *off* the shelves; it can only be seen as a place where "self" was hidden.

But, "Oh little boy, oh little boy," sings Kaspar the wandering mage in *Amahl and the Night Visitors*, proffering his magic box and urging you closer drawer by drawer, through precious stones and shining beads, "in the third drawer I keep . . ." There in my one closet, up at the very top, under sweaters, blankets, boxes not even mine, in a flat paper bag taken down only at night, a half-dozen neatly pressed, desperately hoarded copies of *Physique Pictorial* and *Studio Guild* male posing magazines.

I've often described this developmental period as clinically schizophrenic—not personally but structurally, as it figures in many others' similar processes. By day I was popular, scholarly enough, hetero affective (with a girlfriend named Wendy), elaborately, *meticulously* friendly. After dark, alone, in secret terrible conference, the sailors, surfers, and costumed farmboys, with sweat-oiled bodies and semi-transparent briefs, posed for my singular review. No penis since (there have been hundreds) has encapsulated such perfect promise as those that lay beneath these thin cotton posing straps, which in their veiled seductive power revealed only and exactly as they hid. (This was long before hardcore porn with its poor clinical specificity.) Textile gourmand, I could search my adult life in vain for cotton that delicate and elastic. I outlined the tracings of dick after dick, connoisseur of *chiaroscuro* and *sfumato*:

Hollywood studio light. I masturbated madly, devotedly, now purple with love's wound.

   In the morning I knew nothing. I couldn't tell you, couldn't have told you, how the magazines got back in their cage, and if you'd asked me not only would I have denied knowing about them, but I wouldn't have been able to find them if I tried—and I wouldn't have been lying. I knew nothing.

   And yet, the following Saturday night, after visiting a pretend-beatnik coffeehouse with my best friend Roger, I waved goodbye on my pale green Lambretta motor scooter and veered eastward into darker territory, where a seedier Los Angeles emitted the fumes of over-the-hill actors trapped in their big toupees and small bungalows. Here the all-night, free-for-all Hollywood Ranch Market kept a side room magazine gallery containing racks of specialty journals: my forbidden fruit. With dissembling ease that couldn't have fooled the beetle-like clerk, whose helmet of black plastic hair might have hidden Valentino in decline, I walked the aisle scanning fiercely, face nonchalant, pulse inflamed. At the turn I bravely swallowed my galloping eros which swallowed my galloping shame, quickly perused the appropriate covers and snagged a prize. His face was every dreamed-of face from Kalamazoo or Kansas City; down below innocence met experience in a translucent weave. I threw my money to Valentino, tucked the magazine under arm and

ran out the door. The hooves of my galloping pur-
suers—guilt, exile, eternal loneliness—thundered at my
heels. I jumped on the Lambretta and hit the kick-start.
<u>Night's swift dragons</u> bore me home.

❖ ❖ ❖

"Leland," said the director to our assembled group of
dramaphiles who'd already been in several of his plays,
"I want you to try out for Oberon." A number of us, of
course, would audition for the same part. Leland was
thrilled. He was a brilliant director and actor even then.
His doughy white skin and accelerated hairline made
him look like an adult. A fey, savvy air lifted him seemingly unconcerned above the clawings of the social
crowd, but it was many years before I learned that by the
age of 16 he'd already been arrested in a Beverly Hills
public toilet for having sex—so his savvy air was savvier
than we knew.

"Julie, you study Hermia. Larry. I know you want
Bottom, but take a look at Lysander." Larry, whose
father was a famous comedian and who himself was a
gifted mimic and comic actor, was visibly displeased. He
could out-shtick anyone, and Bottom was the clown
supreme of this play.

"Aww. Come on." He threw in a Jimmy Stewart face
to plead his case.

"Just try it out!" Snap. Snap. With his tight jaw and crocodile grin the director was hard to counter; we knew we could audition for anything we wanted but were better off following his pointed lead.

"Aaron, I want you to try out for Puck."

"Puck?"

"Yes."

"Not Oberon?"

"Do as you wish, but I think you should take a look at Puck." Snap. Snap.

By now I'd swept my cape along enough imaginary promontories as to be seriously deflated—and I *owned* the flower soliloquy—but I went home and thought things through.

I'd never even considered the part of Puck; Oberon with his eloquent high verse and sorcerer's bearing was my natural inclination, or so I'd supposed. Long ago I'd rigged up my bathrobe to suspend from my shoulders as Mandrake the Magician, and I could memorize rhymed lines twenty at a time and spin them from my happy honeyed tongue in public or private. But Puck? Who was that?

If you look at me in photos from this period, my body is delicately thin, my impish nose turned-up, my cheekbones high, my Mongol eyes slanted upwards mischievously, my small ears bat-like and similarly alert. There was something swift and airborne in my features, though

I was woefully unathletic, grounded. An adolescent, monkeying spark remained around the edges of my smile and glinted from my eyes in three-quarters and profile.

Puer Aeternus. Clearly Mr. Ingle saw something I didn't; I was too busy being a boy as a boy to be eternally so. But who could now say he wasn't prescient? There are poetic forms that precede us, just as coded DNA widens the bulb of a nose or flattens the feet.

To put on the mask of a mythic structure that would prove to be my natural face . . .

To mouth the masque of a mythic structure of language whose amped sonorities and playfulness would prove to be my natural voice . . .

Act II, Scene I. A wood near Athens. Puck leaps onto a rock, addresses the creature known (in our production) as 1st Fairy.

"How now spirit. Whither wander you?"

The scene is otherworldly, the dialogue bristling with wings, spangled moonlight, bee pollen. My ears were whirring. Energy streamed in anecdote and couplet. I crooked my knees into a crouch. My voice pitched itself to calibrate the pressure of trickery and instant flight. <u>I am that merry wanderer of the night</u>.

▫ ▫ ▫

Six months earlier I'd attended a banquet for a so-called honor service organization, though I'm not sure what we ever did except raise and lower the school's flag. Privileged among the sons of privilege, we wore black sweaters with white Maltese crosses, and behaved decorously.

Next to me a football player with a penis face—tight, membranous skin and swollen muscularity—made a joke and instead of slapping his thigh slapped mine. The hand stayed. From time to time it raised itself to eat and from time to time it returned to squeeze me above the knee. Conversation around the table continued as if it were normal; below the table his hand found the tender portions of my thigh and massaged them. I believe I swallowed my food. I pretended to myself that I was merely shocked. A thousand jack-off sessions were born—though in the morning I knew nothing, nothing.

I'd been branded, burned, set on fire, seen, toyed with, almost awakened, clamped, made sore, and primed. There's a Courbet painting in the Musée d'Orsay called "L'homme blessé." Perhaps a self-portrait, a dreamy young man with wild hair leans ecstatically against a tree. Evidently, he's been stabbed; if so he's in a transport of pain like St. Sebastian's. His drained, milky complexion is void of tension. The delirium is voluptuous, lifting, consummate. I leaned against my tree torn and exhausted. <u>The bolt of Cupid fell . . . upon a little western flower, now purple with love's wound</u>.

▣   ▣   ▣

"The outlook wasn't brilliant for the Mudville nine that day"—"Casey at the Bat," colloquially iambic; "Listen my children and you shall hear/ Of the midnight ride of Paul Revere"—"Paul Revere's Ride," horsy dactylic; "'Twas a balmy summer evening and a goodly crowd was there,/ Which well-nigh filled Joe's barroom on the corner of the square"—"The Face upon the Barroom Floor," folkloric iambic, with the melodramatic climactic flourish I adored: "With a fearful shriek, he leaped and fell across the picture— dead!" By the age of thirteen I'd memorized all these narrative rhyming ballads and more, derived from a treasured, abject volume called *Best Loved Poems of the American People.*

My real introduction into the art of poetry came through the absorption and recitation of these tired masterpieces. Pursued into adulthood, this pleasure has enabled me to offer you the ten or twenty opening lines of *The Canterbury Tales* in Middle English, of Dante's *Inferno* in the vulgar tongue and *The Iliad* in Homeric Greek, where my staff, a spoon, will mark the hexameters of *Atreides, te anax andron kai dios Achilles,* "Atreus's son [Agamemnon], the king of men, and godlike Achilles." Recitation in public or private, its performative self-dazzlement, reveals poetry's ancient relation to the hypnotic chorus and amphitheater, where Shakespeare's caterpillar may be found munching.

To have taken into my body the riverbank of flowers where Titania slept was to perform Oberon, whether or not I played Puck. The hothouse syllabary was a mage mantra to last me a lifetime. Puck's language, itself, has energy and ticklish response, is filled with roguish anecdote, vertical excitement. Beyond that, when one performs in a play one experiences in the body's echo chamber the language of all the roles. In verse, the brain's muscle memory sets the encased skeleton vibrating, an experience that can only be described as holistic. Among the language arts, poetry is the one most interested in the body, encoding in its formal lexicon methods auditory, circulatory, and neurological.

"Blows/ grows," "woodbine/ eglantine," "night/ delight." The narrative suspense of rhyme—a brief caesura in the middle of action—we could call it the in or out stroke of a fuck; the tease with promise of completion; the organic trace-beats of breath, of course, of pulse and heart; the ear's discrimination of vocalic contour and nuance (Pound's "the tone leading of vowels"); the mathematical or biomorphic imprint of a mind coming to order in constituent parts; the labial/dental grip and spit of consonants in pattern; mnemonic recurrence, hunt and rest, excursion and return, theme and variation; the finger-joints and primal footwork of meter; the muscle torque of bent syntax; the running-animal print of repetitive stress, tug of accent and fall; the oral fixation of pronunciation or the textual shadow of pronunciation so that the senses of the mouth, especially, are awakened; the entire body's pursuance of the senses of the mouth, infantile ecstatic, and so the whole body thrumming to beat, rhyme, phonemic contour, rest, pull, and mental heat. Ignition, paroxysm, swoon.

When I came to study ancient Greek in the 1980s—a fellowship born out of New College in San Francisco who met weekly to learn the language by translating *The Iliad* line by line—"What the hell was happening last night?" asked my downstairs neighbor till he realized the day and knew it was the pride of nine chanting in unison by lamplight—I found the fluid hexameters so riveting I couldn't sleep. Without any semantic content, without even sound, Homer's dactyls, trochees, and spondees imprinted themselves as a moving pattern in my mind so that I lay awake hearing the empty, shifting, mnemonic beat.

Platonic lines of Homeric verse.

I was a terrible young and younger actor, having little sense of character and no wisdom to listen. Language's operations entranced me. I could say I declaimed the parts rather than acted them; my oratorical skills had me caressing each word outside of sense, intoxicated, by which I might pursue it with the soul of love.

Poetry is that literary form in which both the depth function and the surfaces of language are activated, and, pleasures abounding, you are constantly threatened with being in one at the expense of the other. There is no rest. To be in a poem is to live in that constant peril by which meaning is transferred in and out of its form, language performing sensual, decorative, counter-semantic moves just as it absorbs them into structures of content. "Luscious woodbine," and "sweet musk roses" would break away from the very bank in which they're planted, as the reader, "lulled in these flowers", loses his "odoriferous" way. Narrative information gathering and dissemination pretend to architectural stability; the terrible pleasure of verse is to heighten the mutual tension, to dare to undo coherence by agitating sensory display. The whole unit is tougher and more durable for the stress. To ride this contradictory wave in balance is to read a poem in poetry's mode. In and out of presence, appearing and disappearing: The vow of poets attends such elegant suspension as sport, where we are spirits of another sort.

▫   ▫   ▫

Oberon and Puck, a larger and a smaller sprite, the actor and the act. Oberon's poetic disquisitions lead to Puck's swift maneuvers. Cousins to Prospero and Ariel, they're largely Shakespearean inventions, though their antecedents are historically numerous and global.

Puck, the goat boy, a Dionysus in short pants, an eros-nexus of liaisons and sex tricks, thrower of voices, adopter of personae, jokester and piping Pan, turner of day into night. Oberon, his larger self, the shape-shifter and hallucinator, drug maker, spell-binder, Adamic namer of plants, master of the Orphic alphabet who creates the visible world out of the invisible, whose verse is a universe, <u>King of Shadows</u>.

I must admit that as rehearsals began I was flummoxed as to how to play Puck, since my grasp of character was limited, and my body inhibited. I galumphed from rock to rock, listless, arms dragging.

"Do something with your hands," said Mr. Ingle in the early read-through to see how the parts fit us. I flapped a little, timidly.

"No, like this. Hold them up to your face." He spread his fingers and fluttered his hands a bit, as if wings were slowly beating, or as if streaming air around a creature in flight were careening now this way, now that. I made a few clumsy attempts that would certainly have dented my head on a hanging branch or two, but after a while I was relatively airborne. A darting, flickering motion began to emerge.

Leland inflated his already-grand gestures and stentorian voice. The bigger fag by far—or as yet the one true one—he whipped around his invisible cape as if he were in a bullfight, wild enough to sever the heads of a dozen fairies in a swoop. Later, when the black-as-night cape was actually fixed to his narrow shoulders, he would spend most of his time trying not to step on it and fall to the flower-strewn rocks below. I squatted, half in imitation of an elf, and half to clear the arc of this swinging decapitator.

We read through our parts. This was before the cardboard trees became a magical forest, before the slippers, before the beautiful ass's head with giant doe eyes was affixed, before my green vine-clad costume emerged with one leg and one arm cut out, so that leaves, spangled and glittered, circled the right ankle, wound around the torso, and escaped, twining, over the left wrist. How to keep this fluid contraption attached to my body would become an ongoing question, but this was before then, before my balls were tickled and tickled again by the too-intrigued costumer as the sequined vines grew closer and closer to my nervous crotch, sending pheromones <u>through the glimmering night</u>. The play in its entirety unfolded line by line, before I said "Yes," before the slipper, before the announcement of the raked stage.

I should add that in the end my Puck leaned heavily on Roddy McDowell's Ariel, which I'd seen on TV, a gayer-than-air interpretation that spoke to my emerging possibilities and natural inclination. Let's say my cloven

hooves had high arches. They would prove to be pivotal
<u>while these visions did appear.</u>

□   □   □

"I want all of you here to begin rehearsals at 4 o'clock.
We're going to have a raked stage, and you'll have to
learn how to walk on it without falling on your face."

"What's a rake stage?"

Mr. Ingle showed us the maquette, where an
embankment pitched straight up from the footlights at
a 30° angle.

"You can slip and crack your head in a second, so I
want you to practice wearing these." He dangled from
his hand a crumpled black thing, claw-like.

"What is it?"

"They're ballet slippers, and they'll keep you from
sliding all over the place. You have to move elegantly,
lightly, and you'd better start now. There are boxes in the
foyer. Find a pair that fits today."

Ballet slippers! I tried to unscrew the damaged look
from my face. Balls of lead attached themselves to my
toes and stomach, as I crawled like a dying gnome up
the aisle. Ballet slippers? It was a bit of semiotics I had-
n't reckoned with in April 1965.

I wasn't naive. Though in the mornings I knew nothing, I was well aware of Leland's proclivities if not his

actions, and my brother, one giant step ahead, had already brought home from his new apartment in Hollywood a slender young blond with a glamorous fold of hair combed impeccably down his forehead into his eyes that almost had my father running for his gun. I'd been popular; I'd been elected to offices; I held position. In short, I was very well protected, armored right up to my elfin ears with social power, social grace. I could collapse this noble house with one stretch of my delicate foot.

I chose a box and contemplated the contents: two viciously nesting bats. I dangled one from my fingers— it was thin elasticized cotton with a white suede-like sole. I opened it from its curl to better imagine the fit.

"Fag!"

I looked at my foot and then at the slipper.

"Queer!"

My assembled friends—and *every* football player— bore down on me with unveiled contemptuous jeers.

"Look at the fairy!"

Beyond every other action in, of, or around the play, I knew what wearing these little black shoes would mean. About *myself* I knew nothing as yet—line stretched thin to breaking—but how others would read me was inevitable. The codes and their cataclysmic rewards were long fixed in place.

I took a few hundred breaths and felt the rhythm flow.

"<u>I know a bank</u>," I said to myself, "<u>where the wild thyme blows</u>." I lifted my feet; the high arches promised sure-footedness and balance.

"Sissy," whispered the empty box, but I batted it aside.

I pointed my foot and wiggled my toes and meditated on them for days, while climbing vines encircled me <u>with sweet musk roses and with eglantine</u>. Carefully, with metrical ease, I slipped into the shoe. It was a natural fit. I straightened my spine and took a step; the grip held. Testing the measure, I paced the foyer wall to wall. Leland, Julie, and Larry were already rehearsing.

<u>Quite overcanopied with luscious woodbine</u>, I walked quietly down the aisle to the bustling stage, where I would prove to be a mild sensation as Puck in the Beverly Hills High School senior production of *A Midsummer Night's Dream* in May of 1965.

Later that month—it couldn't have been more than three weeks after the play closed—I met a man in a Boston dormitory who twinkled at me ceremoniously and invited me to his room. His hair curled tight like a satyr and his eyes were <u>nodding violets</u>.

I answered, "Yes," as though it were a casual response, "Yes, absolutely."

The normal ones had all gone to sleep, safe in their flannel sheets. The night was silent, <u>glimmering</u>. I stood in the doorway by his small bunk bed; in the morning

I'd know everything, everything. He slid me a long, mischievous smile and stretched out his arms. "<u>Take hands with me</u>," he prompted tenderly . . .

"<u>and rock the ground whereon these sleepers be</u>."

Sunlight is an enclosure, but with a view. You get situated in space as heat expands your generous sense of being there, inscribed into a locus by the warming sun's weight. I sit on an exposed log in the park. The variegated shades of green are lavish for January; the clarified warmth would be remarkable, too, any place else but here.

Acacias are the most forward with a yellow propelling their green leaves, a forecast of the fuzzy blooms that'll soon stink up the hillside. I saw a few pink plum blossoms popping on their branches, and just now an early nervous hummingbird twitter and streak. I could claim everything I see as somehow mine; in other words I have the chance to invest it all with meaning.

Over there on the crag-top known as Corona Heights five figures assemble in two groups, standing at a level higher than my vantage point, with a considerably broader view—but far less settled in than I. My fallen tree-trunk is a through line: It extends me horizontally to the left and to the right, anchors me with its deep memory of the vertical, and lets me balance securely with my legs dangling like a fisherman at peace with empty expectation. To be at rest outside but not in the wild like this, in a city familiar and local but wild like this—the hawks shriek and plow the air just above the bush-tops—to be stationed under a sunny sky in a zone so open yet so delineated—perimeters inside of perimeters—with senses alert but utterly stabilized is to be in a kind of home. And that is why birds perch.

I watched a large red-tailed hawk yesterday land ten feet away on a lowish branch by a path, where he was unusually close to the ground but beautifully disguised as a clump of pine-cones and needles. He sat in an arboreal thicket but the space around him was round. I detoured *onto* the path to arrive practically beneath him. His silhouette almost obliterated his features, but I soon discerned the squat head turned to me. I'd approached carefully from behind, but there he was, calm but riveted, focused directly my way, with an almost impossible muscular twist since his body was facing exactly the opposite direction.

I walked the path to get another angle on the view of him; he continued to follow my every step, completing, without shifting his feet, what had to be a 360° rotation. The hawk possessed a sphere of himself, then, with his eyes and his beak at the center of an observed proprietary world. He'd made a poised place at the focal point inside a shifting circumference of sight, I'll say, and calmly interpreted the outer circle according to his needs and predilection. I parted as a marginal threat not too seriously taken, to return to whatever peripheries awaited me. It's the closest by far I've been to a wild hawk. That *he* owned *me* was never in doubt, and I left whistling.

MORNING IN THE VALLEY

The placement has bright, sharp sun inside of a cool breeze; late fall sycamores, mulberries, poplars, deciduously; layers of receding hillsides, evergreen into gray. A stillness that is sanctuary. (Does the obvious lack of distracting sound increase the agility of sight, so that you notice more, penetrate farther?) A few hysterical squawks—woodpecker—from the treetops. The old pendulous fig tree has gone yellow; its gigantic leaves—sixteen inches across—plop onto the surface of the warm pool.

An overstuffed white and yellow cat that belongs to the resort met me at the door to my room as I returned with morning coffee. He nudged his head between my feet and the screen door to get in, but my allergy rebuffed him. His eyes were completely communicative—I have to say they *spoke*—with that balance of emotion and intellect that equals intimate conversation. When I went out he was pre-possessively still there, meeting my gaze directly, following me to the stair's edge. As I turned back to catch his face between slats of the balcony rail—I really *liked* him even though I didn't want to touch him—he flipped his eyes from mine to the sky in a trajectory so swift I couldn't be sure it happened. His pretense to indifference was total. Being caught looking backward—the mournful past—was not something he was willing to permit.

I take my cue from the cat and try looking at the sky. The Hot Springs here encourage spiritual perspective, so I raise my eyes against the tentacles of the last few months: disappeared boyfriend, over-committed workplace, national warmongering, free-floating anxiety. The Northern California sky is as empty as the present is, as full. A clean wash of blue gathers toward white in the crotch of the distant hills. ["The sky covered the sky."]

There seem to be two sets of separate, sequential lenses on my eyes (a woodpecker's hammering on a sycamore): one for the present and one for the past, immediacy and mediation. A cute guy walks by. (I watched him do yoga on the redwood deck yesterday afternoon. His body's an urban primitive canvas of torso-wide geometric tattoos; his pierced dick's weighed down by an alarmingly large silver ring.) I can see now that the extended pictographic lines across his back and shoulders are the wing bones of what I *think* is the skeleton of a pterodactyl, whose body of pure bone is suspended from the nape of this guy's neck. The archaic—no, the archeological!—conjoins the contemporary. It's a yogic crucifix of startling elasticity fusing his agile arms to his vertebrae, wing and foundation, his whole moving figure shadowed by a prehistoric transparency. (Last night I kept thinking, "What do we call those dudes with all the tattoos and piercings?" I couldn't locate the phrase I wanted. "Neo Geo?" No, that's painting. "Neo Tribal?" Nope. When I found the correct "Urban Primitive" it seemed both exactly right and entirely too tame for a desiccated, reanimated, pterodactyl-man. "Neoclassic Jurassic?")

One eye fixed and one eye wandering, like the great strange-sighted poet Robert Duncan, whose stationary crossed right eye seemed to hold you down like a hawk's claw for dissection or delectation, while the operative left went rummaging through history to provide you with a thorough backdrop and context. A lot of poets I know use Zen as a compositional model, as if writing truly could enact a current stream of attention. But the writer searching through lexicon is always at least a synapse away, not only because language is a medium of mediation but because the writer is also a reader, casting an eye to formal elements coming into coherence, and this stereoscopic cross-transport is a fusion of temporal zones, the doing, the just-did, the going-to-do. Composition's a trans-present, co-informed by memory, the immediate local, and the imagination. (A gray cat I didn't see because I was writing cries at my elbow; because I was writing my distance perception was dislocated and

I thought the screech was a blue jay across the pool, then a child over by the small deck. I cocked my head and turned to the distances; a second cry brought me down to the chair I'm sitting in where the complaining cat slinks three inches below my writing arm.)

The narration and its parentheses: Can they be one continuous movement and can I remain permeable to their shifts? My anger at ex-boyfriend Willie was a disjunct transposition of the past onto, *into,* the present, so that I was infected by a series of jagged, incomplete rehearsals—wounding moment; fantasy accusations; fabulous, bitter retorts. Four months later, December envelops me with the calculated terms of release: You feel your multiple senses come to a point in the brain where they unify, a *sentience.*

When I watched the tattooed man do yoga a sympathetic magic took hold of me. His extensions were extraordinary, his fluid positions articulate to the tips of his digits. I seemed to go into his contemplative world where a muscular and skeletal precision signified total inhabitation of place, and my own body, which had been reading, felt his multiphasic, gyroscopic, twisting arc and swoop. *To concentrate, to participate, to coalesce, to inscribe, to occupy, to enact.*

For the sake of compositional accuracy I pick up my books and towels and go looking for the illustrated man, to find out what the pterodactyl image *really* is. I want to ground my fancy in his imagination. But he's nowhere to be found, of course; he's gone from the valley, gone home. I'm left with the image that I've constructed, *my* ideogram, *my* remedial tattoo. It broadens my shoulders and aligns my back, a corrective wingspan of meditative synthesis. Taken from his torso it fits me like a fact.

   I flex the page and stretch.

THREE SCENES FROM THE SAUNA
AT THE YMCA

The old man in the sauna with failing eyes squints shamelessly to see the lean young thing sitting four feet across from him. I've seen this old guy before with his lost-his-glasses face and hanging skin. Today he's drying himself endlessly—the sauna heat must have him dripping as fast as he's drying—so he can shimmy his towel across his back forever gazing dumbfounded at the seemingly oblivious stud. I've never seen anyone squint like this man does: The whole apparatus of his face seems to deflate. It opens rather than tightens, an ovoid slack that makes him look dazed, as if he were being blinded instead of sighted. In this unnerving blindness I'm thinking it's himself that he can't see. His nose and cheeks and chin diminish in his leering in favor of eyes that widen, emptying their contents and making him look childlike in their single-minded yet vague focus. His ass, I see, is tiny like mine will be and his back and shoulders bristle with long white hairs that are almost erect. Slack jawed and loosened up, some pure pursuit of waning pleasure pulls him. He carries a smile on that divination—it's projection—he sees what he wants to see—there are suggestions and outlines—nobody else can see him he's blown away riding a wind or a current of remembered sex—if he can't really see he can't really be seen—the foolishness is reserved for those looking at him not him looking at them he remains *inside* the regard as a component of the persistent, revolving lure.

▫   ▫   ▫

In this same YMCA sauna I watched a pugnacious little guy (my sense was a Boston Irish tough) fiddle with himself across the bench from me in a way that almost resembled the cruising gestures (and more) that are frequent and sometimes desirable in this sharp-scented wooden box. Others were there and I couldn't quite get the picture. We were most of us naked; he had his hand over his genitals as if he were pushing them down, which was something slightly different than the usual lengthening pull considered a come on for obvious reasons. He came and went a couple of times and I couldn't complete the picture which wouldn't settle or cohere. There was no seduction in the little room, I could feel that I couldn't feel it. He was a small tough guy, barking at someone on the bench above to move his feet so he could sit. I looked as I didn't look I needed a completing piece. The curly hair, his scruffy, wiry beard, slim but rough-and-ready torso. I saw two lines upwards diagonal running from beneath his nipples, long scars where breast tissue had been removed. I looked back at his dick without looking: His hands still pushed slyly down to keep the disobedient skin pendulous: something two-dimensional, a suggestion rather than a fact. I didn't need another clue I couldn't see. This is the ultimate male province, I thought, locker room and showers in an urban YMCA, made maler by the gay sex that always did or didn't happen. The courage and daring trapeze flight without a net of this person delighted me. Though it took me fifteen minutes to decode I considered his victory complete.

◻   ◻   ◻

A guy next to me is handsome, swarthy, lean—but he's uptight in a silly masculine way: "dude" or "hey, man." His cock is nice, though it doesn't grow as he flirts with me and makes me flirt with him. He repositions slightly, inches closer along the steam room's wet shelf. They've been running this thing so hot you can barely see and I can barely see his dick which isn't growing as he touches my foot with his foot like an accident but intentionality is a foregone conclusion. He plays with my foot with his foot and doesn't remember we did this once before. He smiles at me furtively through the steam though it's a weak little smile not a sly one because he's carrying shame in a way that stifles pleasure. It gets too hot, I leave and shower; we reconvene in the dry sauna. He's sitting across from me and rests his foot on the wooden slats surrounding the heating mechanism. I'm not sure what he wants, what to do. He says, "Put your foot up." I stretch and as if it were comfortable and as if it were something I wanted to do place my foot so it's facing his. He makes them meet like they're mirror images and softly moves his sole over mine. His cock is no bigger and neither, now, is mine. There's something too deliberate, too narrowly fetishistic in this gesture in a place where wilder things happen routinely. Later when we're drying off and dressing I invite him over to capitalize on the foreplay. "Hey, man, thanks, but I've got to go shop for dinner." Another time, I say—and realize I've been had: Footsies must equal third base to this dude. I consider my feet which have completed him, and drive home leaning on their shame and the delicious certainty of having been used.

BLUE IN GRAY

There's a certain amount of projection inevitable in social circumstances (how to enact simultaneous subject/object awareness is an unsolvable conundrum), and I carry into the bar with me this dueling disposition: wanting to appear reasonably seductive, but feeling inconsolably overblown. There's my own discomfort at being single and suffering the pressure of having or needing to go to a gay bar to meet someone at this late date, along with the prickly awareness that I'm glaringly at least twenty years older than most of the other men—as evidenced by my weary impatience, my utter disinterest in getting publicly drunk, and most troublingly by the rapidly-growing salt in the fading pepper of my hair.

"Here's the scenario," I tell Susan one afternoon, then Norma and Rob the next day, and I tell Ben, too, the following night because who wants to be alone with their misery *or* their cleverness?—"I walk into one of these crowded places and it's like I'm a husk of a person, just a moving sheaf of clothing suspended from a top-knot of white hair."

"Come on; there's some gray. You look fabulous."

"Thank you," I nod without appreciation, "but I'm

69

not talking about that, I mean what it seems like, what I read into them from watching their eyes, what I *see* they're thinking—and I'm *sure* they are." ("Yes, feelings, not facts," adds Susan in her up-to-date therapist's phraseology.) "I go into a bar and if I introduced myself it'd be, 'Hi, my name is White Hair, what's yours?'"

My friends give me that don't-be-ridiculous look, with just a barely visible alarm under the surface at my evident distressed mood. Rob, whose hair has basically left the playing field, kindly tolerates my inflated drama and demurs: "I assure you nobody thinks that. You look great."

But for once I'm not fishing for compliments. In the bar I'll shift impatiently from wall to wall, corner to corner, doorframe to bench, trying to fill out an empty space, to be present in absence, to get moderately comfortable standing invisible under my radiant halo. I'll swig my one beer at faster and faster intervals, peeling the soggy label like a hound pawing a hole in the earth, because what else is there to do with your hands or your lips at this silent juncture, lit up like a lamppost yet wholly unseen?—and wait embarrassed in the smoldering shadows for the last drops that'll signal my time to leave: I did my part, I tried, I went *out!*

At home I remember with a start that my maternal grandfather—they're *his* genes—died with a full head of silver hair. Will I ever go back to the bar with this flashlight on my head or just stay at home frozen in the gleam of my thinking cap, my icicle yarmulke, my blizzard at the summit, blinding shockwave, shining conflagration, my personal cloud of sighs, this percolating steam vent, the "flag of my disposition," as Whitman has it, my unloved tiara in false possession supplanting my righteous name . . . !

A DISCOVERY

"Go through all the drawers and cupboards. He must have made out a will."

The rooms have that sealed-off kind of parental neatness, as if life happened tentatively *among* the chests and chairs rather than on or in them. Bad china, cheap silver, an old samovar not really worth its tea; some kitschy wall décor; miscellaneous papers and a few of my father's busted bank books full of zeros. On top of the blond buffet a gilded head of Frank Sinatra: "Caesar's Palace xxx Anniversary/ Ol' Blue Eyes." Turn it over—surprise, it's a music box: "*I did it my wa-ay.*"

But no will. Nothing to straighten out the mess. No help from beyond the grave: a neat, complete escape.

"It isn't like him; there has to be one." Contents are emptied on the living room floor, garbage for gulls.

Then the small top drawer of a bureau opens its mouth. No legal papers, but an orderly pack of same-size yellow notes or tickets, bound by a rubber band.

"What the hell are these?" I ask.

My brother and I rifle through the imposing stack. *Eagles by seven. Colts by three. Rams by ten.* $200. $100. $200. $50. $20. $200. A pile of ten-pick football stubs, one ruined projection after another, "twenty-five, thirty, thirty-five, forty, fifty, sixty, seventy . . ."—the bookie's seaside condo and Porsche. In the end, a single year's desperate miscalculations: $200,000 lost.

We look at each other, incredulous; my "uncle" Harold tries to look at the wall. That my father had gambled before we were born we all knew. That he'd continued to do so right up to his death—wasted on wheeling and dealing and in debt—we'd had no idea. We sit in the middle of the floor, tickets spread before us like a misaligned tarot deck reading the past instead of the future.

I want to say the discovery—the *telling*—of this stack of cards became the meaning of my father's threnody, the true text of the poem of his death. Our fraternal shock and release: the matrix of partial answers; his unprovoked brutality, incessant desperation, angry phone calls, no phone calls, disownings, rages; the willfulness, obsession, disregard, abuse, and vanity; the self-inflicted isolation, the heart attacks, the amputations, the brute force, the bile, were newly revealed as matter in the spinal weave of the last poem's uncovered imperative. The subjective territory I had weathered, the theme I'd long been working (the same list: brutality, phone calls, rages, etc.) was only now properly configured in the unfolding composition of his obituary.

⊞   ⊞   ⊞

I'm impelled to turn this small recursive narrative from the paternal edge and raise corresponding elements of discovery in my practice of poetry, where the poem's everyday agenda is to read the world's hidden text of correspondences. Where the material is not necessarily grim, as above, but *is* necessarily mortal: "It is difficult/ to get the news from poems/ yet men die miserably every day/ for lack/ of what is found there"—Williams. Where the material is, in fact, unknown until it is met, the matter is dross until it is formed, the subject moot until it is subject to creative forces.

To write in poetic mode as a *discoverer* is to follow each word and its interior monologue of semantic nuance, to test each word in juxtaposition of sequence and collective order coming into structural reverberation and pattern recognition. To empty all the drawers in order to find what you weren't looking for, the sad radiant clue of absolution. One epitaph from Emerson: "We study to utter our painful secret."

To write in poetic mode as a discoverer is to patiently house a biomorphic disposition, an itch in the mind, a disequilibrium that is an urge toward clarification or expression, at once a lack and an excess. It's a means by which a community of vital interests is visited upon the mononuclear family of meaning, by which etymological resource is laid into language by sound, fiction and fact undergo binocular fusion, and at last a paternal secret is returned to the father as a son's bruise made vivid and forgiven in a field of resonances.

The mood is October. I'm contemplating my poetic practice, jogged by a memory after my father's death that rewrote our history, an unsought discovery with the power to move forwards and backwards, and finally hold his constellation of behavioral urges in place. A process of creative awakening that could have provided him—as it did us—with the necessary structural evidence to keep him standing.

He would have had to find it seeking anything.

With a second epitaph from Emerson: "The thought and the form are equal in the order of time."

THE PEOPLE'S P***K
A Dialectical Tale

As part of my literary biography, I often joke to those in the know that I'm the bastard son of Robert Duncan and Frank O'Hara, an heir to seemingly irreconcilable poetic territories: diction high and low; mythopoeic drama and breezy, urban rhythm; Esclarmonde de Foix in her holy fortress and Lana Turner in her turban; sweet, communal San Francisco and vigorous, imperial New York (I was born and raised as a child in Manhattan, have lived my adult life in S.F.). But the truth is I'm the lovechild of Denise Levertov and Robert Duncan. Each was my longtime poetic mentor, teacher, beloved friend, spiritual guide, and muse. For each I was apprentice, acolyte, amanuensis, confidant, communer, and fellow traveler.

From early 1969, when I met Denise, to Robert's death in 1988, they were the highest comrades of my poetic community; their work awakened me to the power and possibility of American poetry, and called me forward into my own imagination and practice. If our friendships swelled or faded as did their own, mastery notwithstanding, the work was resolute. Such graces of encounter are not casual. As in the familial paradigm (Robert died the same year as my father), individuation is the synthesis of deep obedience and disavowal: In the crisis of these poets' unfolding esthetic and political conflict my own writing was tested and proved—and still is.

▣   ▣   ▣

In the spring of 1969 I was nearing the end of my undergraduate days at Berkeley, a tenure reaching from the close of the Free Speech Movement (in which my brother Isak, to whom Levertov's "Relearning the Alphabet" is dedicated, was arrested) through vivid, multiple protests against the Viet Nam buildup, conscription, and university racism, along with various unnamed armed conflicts (my 21st birthday found me under curfew-driven house arrest as National Guardsmen patrolled each civic corner; I remember the fact, but who can remember the reason why?) as well as through the Summer of Love, the great Human Be-in, The Fillmore, the Avalon, Hendrix, and Joplin; through, too, uncountable nights charting my own adventurous forlorn and ecstatic forays into gay life in the city; all seeming to culminate, then, in the epochal war-at-home known as the battle for People's Park. How can the spring of 1969 in Berkeley be registered without such coordinates, the *feel* of cultural seismology and the pressure of localized national events? So when Denise's poetry class answered the call to come work at People's Park, each of those historical ganglia was waving, charged, and for each of us, I think, symbolic action was fed by these cumulative empowerments and disempowerments.

It must have been a bright sunny day, that 14th of May Denise describes in "Staying Alive," because I remember the sheen on the green as we rolled out great swaths of sod like a carpet to cover the ground of the park. The school quarter had been peppered with demonstrations and student strikes, and we'd often, if I remember correctly, met off-campus; that we should go together to work at the park was testimony to our support of Denise's political conviction as well as our belief that the common purposes of poetry made a place for voice in the space of action; "the personal is political" extended its alliterative syllogism to include "poetry." Denise describes scooping up debris to haul away to a dump, and who could help imagining that a red wheelbarrow might have been involved?

That specific domestic conflict was galvanizing, and in a particularly San Francisco way the poetic community came alive to its civic urgency and called together a resplendent literary gathering to raise money for the park. On Monday, June 2, the great California Hall was the site of an overflowing "Poetry Reading for the People's Park," with appearances by Levertov, Duncan, Brautigan, Ferlinghetti, Snyder, McClure, and others. The scene was raucous, celebratory, serious, committed, with overtones of literary history and an aura of cultural significance, fed by the political drama of the immediate weeks and orchestrated by Denise's role as MC.

What fate, I can almost hear Robert ask, was at work in bringing Denise to that role on that stage that night, where her uses of poetry and her use by poetry met their boundaries and overflowed? The chaotic (post-Beat?) impulses of the Bay Area cultural scene were different than those of the Movement that was framing her current practices, and her sober streak hardened in direct proportion to the gospel-like fervor, the shrieks and laughter, the carnal carnival of the gathered masses. As she felt the crowd inch beyond her control—beyond her intentions, as if the poem itself refused to obey her projections—where she would bring it back to a political formulation exactly as the audience was riding its imagination—a face came over her face that was a borrowed face, a stern righteous visage that wasn't a poetic face yet was exactly what Robert saw or feared he saw as the face of her war poems.

As if on cue, up onto the stage from somewhere in the audience jumped an eight-foot pink felt penis, who grabbed the mike and announced to the crowd that he was "The People's Prick," bouncing around like a giant bunny on LSD. The audience roared its approval (the other operative syllogism extended "free all political prisoners" into "free love")—but not Denise. She was outraged. She was affronted. She knew better. She tried to take back control, hectoring the audience to behave with a puritan, if not Stalinist, regard that made it clear that Emma Goldman's revolution was not *her* revolution. But the *audience* was *not* hers. The Prick defied her, danced around her, as her sense of offence congealed and straightened her unbending spine into something far more disturbingly erect.

I no longer remember how events progressed after that, but for me the image of the clash between the embodied pleasure principle and the officer of the doctrinaire has stood precisely for the poetic trouble Robert envisioned when he cautioned Denise that her public poetic thinking was "a force that, coming on *strong*, sweeps away all the vital weaknesses of the living identity; the *soul* is sacrificed to the demotic persona that fires itself from spirit" [Letter 409], and, later, "The poet's role is not to oppose evil, but to imagine it. . . . Is it a disease of our generation that we offer symptoms and diagnoses of what we are in the place of imaginations and creations of what we are?" [Letter 452] or, even at the very beginning of their correspondence, "The feeling of what is false for me is the evident *use* of language to persuade" [Letter 21]. And how, in the end, can we not be reminded of Duncan's Freudian complaint, which so enraged Denise, that read into the skinned-penises of "Life at War" "an effect and tone of disgusted sensuality."

He would not be alone, here, in registering the break between Movement politics and the socio-political implications of cultural and personal exploration, which found their catalysts in the emerging Women's and Gay liberation movements—even if this insight did not succeed in liberating poetry from the rhetoricizing projections of those very countering insurgencies. Yet there my poetry fled, bounding into the communal arms of gay comrades, who fought both the male domination of the power brokers of the revolution and the homophobia and heterosexism that fed it. The rhetoric was heavy; the poems groaned under its weight. But if I'd understood the problem that lay within the People's Prick scenario, it went only so far as to resurrect (re-erect?) issues of pleasure—the life of Eros and the social registrations of its repression—from the peace movement's cemetery, but not yet entirely to question the poem's obedience to my instructions. The American people's red army may have been mutated, but if you read the poetry in my first book (and you needn't) you will find that I was frequently writing like a new pink officer of the doctrinaire.

The spring of People's Park marked the beginning,

not the end, of my friendship with Denise. In fact, she had given me every sense of poetry's immediacy and magic; the California Hall reading was a small event in a large apprenticeship. We both moved east that summer, and stayed in proximity for years. The finesse of her poetic line—its rhythmic and perceptual discriminations—remains for me, with Creeley's, the definitive American investigative verse line (though the writing I *refer* to largely predates the war poems.) The disciplinarian that seemed in evidence later was not so in evidence earlier; instead there was the most joyful, appreciative, wonder-seeking, and wonder-giving person I'd yet met. This is the same writer Robert adored, a poet whose aural and visual access to a sensory world places her in the company of H.D. and Dickinson, of Colette and Virginia Woolf, a writer capable of an audible hush into which a melodic apprehension of experience is raised precisely into language.

I've found, in rereading letters, that sympathy to gay ideology as it was forming was not intuitive to her, though her sympathy to *me* was, and we discussed in person and through correspondence the arguments and articulations of gender construction and sexual liberation. She was frankly confused, and interested in being educated; from her few responses I must have offered my own (communally derived) convictions and cant about male domination and power. (A letter from 1972 has probing questions from her about homosocial theory, and naive ones about homoerotic formation and even wicked hairdressers.) We visited regularly, and spoke with great emotional intimacy, and each visit for me was a privileged occasion. By the time I moved to San Francisco in the summer of 1974 we'd been in less-frequent contact; a letter sent in '75 shows we'd been out of touch for a while. It contains a reference to the idea of, and the seeds to, her poem "Writing to Aaron," which appeared in *Life in the Forest* and which raised a consonant pang in Robert—"And that's how we lost touch for so long" [Letter 472]. And when, in 1976, my first book was published, I sent it to Denise with expectant pride. The irony of her response was bitter: "Some of your poems are too emphatically homosexual for me to identify with, as you surely realize," she wrote.

> "When I seem to detect a note of propaganda it turns me off completely. But when you are simply writing poetry and transcending opinion then I can respond. This may sound inconsistent from one who has written 'political' poetry, but I believe my political concerns to be less parochial in theme."

Her analysis of dogma infecting my poetry per se could have come right from Robert's critique of her own writing, though the second part was hers alone, and the wound it opened between us was never really healed. She was telling me, in fact, that it wasn't a poetic argument that most mattered to her: The argument was political and revolved around the supremacy of her own ideology. Parochial! If I (thought I) was busy tying up racism, misogyny, homophobia, and warmongering into a unified theory of oppression, her authoritarianism split the weave, and unraveled me where I was most in need of support, where my own personal sense of oppression was, in fact, most tenderly situated. This double face of her response had the power of revelation: of a true homophobia in her nature ("too emphatically homosexual") that called forth the same stern disapproving persona who so vehemently opposed The People's Prick.

▫ ▫ ▫

It occurs to me now that Denise's ruffled recalcitrance may have hidden the fact that I had recently met and formed a friendship with Robert Duncan. I must have told her, and she must have felt in a paranoid way—as she certainly did later—that this new association implied a censure and maybe even a kind of gay alliance.

I'd met Robert on a Market Street trolley in 1975, capping an imaginative sequence begun earlier in the week.

I'd had a dream in which a rainbow loop of light appeared to me on a cliff-top, raising such howling winds that I was nearly driven over. A hand appeared from a nearing car to steady me, and bring me safely into the presence of the enormous, pulsating light. I awoke and named that light "Jehovah," and wrote a poem that seemed to me, then, all my own, with the sense of finding my true way into poetry for the first time. The next day, in a bookstore, I chanced upon *The Opening of the Field,* and opened directly to the poem "A Natural Doctrine," in which a rabbi Aaron of Baghdad "came upon the Name of God and achieved a pure rapture." "But it was for a clearing of the sky . . . my thought cried," writes Robert, and "the actual language is written in rainbows." Just a few days later I spied him on the bus, introduced myself, recounted in the most astonished way the correspondences between my dream and the poem, flush with the magic of circumstance, synchronicity, or fate. I remember distinctly that Robert was unimpressed by the linkage, as if this foretelling were a matter of course, utterly quotidian. But he was just enough impressed with me to invite me to come visit him, which I soon did.

I brought with me my first chapbook publication, and read it aloud; Robert's response was gleeful and warm. The piece united themes of ritual transvestism, gender deconstruction, and plain ol' drag, and even by that time the writing was willing to be "fabulous"—to test the bounds of content permission and diction—in a way that was directly related to my reading of Duncan. His response, and our connection, I would say, was not based on some perceived or evident gay fraternal alliance but rather on this common understanding (my understanding under the wing of his) that the writing would be permitted to go where it needed to go, unabashed. It could never be "too emphatically homosexual" only because it could never be "too" *anything* in terms of limit or censure. This revelatory position in relation to permission was the foundation of my understanding of Robert's poetics, the key to his cosmic orchestrations and orchestral modulations—and remains so.

◻ ◻ ◻

For me, from then, the conflict was resolutely resolved in terms of the poem's form being isometric with its (emerging) content, and a belief that when the poem is infected by the right-thinking politics which is dogma—replacing flexible *at*tention with inflexible *in*tention—it dies on the vine. Though Robert knew of my friendship with Denise, and I remember early on his addressing the issue in terms that were insufficiently clear to me so I may only have nodded sheepish assent, it was not really a subject of our conversation. By the '80s it was clear that Denise was staying away from San Francisco, possibly so as not to have to contend directly with Robert. (A letter from 1980 states "I just can't take that SF scene—was there in secret last summer & don't dig it.")

But then something came into view that challenged *my* political will, that threatened to deliver the politic back into the poetic in a way unmatched in the previous fifteen years: AIDS. By the late '80s AIDS had ravaged San Francisco, seizing the territory of both action and imagination, and how to write about or into AIDS became, for me, an unavoidable confrontation, and challenged explorative composition with its insistence of thematic content. Advocacy, action, information, were demanded; the very nature of the epidemic spewed information and viral activity. At a loss as to how to meet this troubling matter in poetry without resorting to didacticism, I turned to prose to help me carry the more direct addresses—the portraiture and narrative of events—that were consonant with my experience, built largely around the struggles and insights of friends, of "comrades," I want to say, "returning to the rhetoric of an early mode." But when I finally found the means to write complexly about AIDS through poetry it was not dogmatic and was not presumptuously moralizing; the piece ("Human

Immune") carried elegiac weight through a *formal* ideology, built on an epidemiological model: Each stanza grew by design larger than the previous, subsumed it, so that without realizing it the reader was brought *inside* the epidemic, as if surrounded by the virus. And I spoke not from my own first person, but from a range of subject/object, singular, and plural points of view to suggest the invariability of risk and loss. I spoke, in fact, as just such a People's Prick who in an earlier era jumped onstage to announce the pleasure principle, but here the pleasure was inextricably conjoined with pain: "I squirted them with kisses. On his back at the edge of the couch to die of pleasure . . ." To say the words that couldn't be said to address the content that had to be spoken—the sacramental profane—with a phallic imperative, to "penetrate into their historian's hearts and foist upon the reader authenticity of the marvels."

The oracle, whose exact charge was to speak into the unspeakable, had stepped forward and demanded ground. "I want that energy while speaking, place yourselves close by me, excessive behavior swell discourse in proportion." Since the disease itself was not a moral occasion, the poem needed to voice *not-myself* arising from *not-my-moral-circumstance*, and would range in accordance with the full multiphasic ceremony of public and secret acts. The permission I needed to write the poem could not have come from hounding the pene-trating organ off the stage.

    The test and retest of esthetics informed by convic-tions, the vision of art's purposes and possibilities in rela-tion to or *as* action, remain the core processes enacted by—and *engendered* by—the Duncan/Levertov corre-spondence. If sympathy to Robert's poetics excited my own writing, the passionate advocacy and determination to speak into *un*necessary silence I'll trace to both men-tors—and the poetics of their contention is dialectically *in* me. I've only ever counted such dual inheritance as one of extraordinary luck: their immediate graces mine to learn from, their tensions played out in the parame-ters of my work. The spiraling conversation is acute: "A mind hovering ecstatic/ above a mouth in which the heart rises," writes Robert, and Denise will answer, "The poem ascends."

DAHLIAS

I knocked lightly at the classroom door, opened it and peeked my head in. Miss Hendrix saw me, but so, too, did a number of children, with their hyperactive eyes-behind-their-heads and bristling antennae tuned to incoming stimuli. A chorus instantly rang out: "Aaron, Aaron, Aaron; Poetry! Yay! Poetry!"

I've told this story many times, how nobody before and nobody since has quite sparked up like that when I entered a room, and never in my life in any other circumstance did I hear any group actually say, "Yay, poetry!" But these second graders in San Francisco had the charge, and they were the apex of my brief stint teaching for California Poets in the Schools.

Those in the third grade had their own considerable charm, especially one spike-haired Asian American boy named David who always caught my entrance from the opposite end of the long room, racing at me like a torpedo till he took flight and leaped into my arms at the arrival point. He later wrote me what I've always taken to be the best love poem of *my* life, which said, "When Aaron come in. He look like a lovely as the sky. He was as pretty as a clouds. His body look like as soft as a hamster skin."

By the fourth grade I caught a dissonance, and by the fifth I thought I finally understood the paradigm behind the Biblical Fall: These kids had fallen into gender. The boys were now cruel and the girls were blasted, bitter.

Back in the second grade the undifferentiated children were at work on their poetry, dreaming language in newly unfettered ways, and pausing briefly to contemplate. I ranged the room as an accomplice, leaned over and squatted way down next to each student, a few inches away. Then they turned their shining faces up to me—quizzically, or with pride, or just compositional pleasure—and I was flooded with that light they emit, something willing and bright, that lit me, and for which I still hunger, unsatisfied. Later I said to myself, I said to my friends, "They turned their little faces to me like flowers."

⊡   ⊡   ⊡

How is a person like a flower, and who's augmented by the comparison? If a person *is* like a flower, can a flower be like a person? Why doesn't that comparison hold quite as well, and what do we want from them? We were covering an exercise in class (now it's for graduate students in an MFA writing program) on "flora": Go see it, pay attention, describe it. By luck and totally by chance in the middle of my own lesson, I hit Golden Gate Park's dahlia garden in preposterous full bloom. About fifty square yards of outsized, overpetaled, shaggy booming flowers, speckled and striped, ruffled and layered, and speaking colors I've never even known the name of, much less how to evoke. Magenta and mauve? Too Victorian, and too stable. Bright yellow? Too singular, and lacking a thrust of energy. Red? But with black bleeding it. Orange: You must be kidding—this livid, churning, moonlit fire?

The range of dahlia shapes here taxes taxonomy. Some have fluted petals, like rows of curled tongues, that amass in starched collars and speak Dutch. Some have the blowzy overdetermination of kings and queens, mighty, almost-weary figureheads overhanging their propping stalks, those plebeian supporters. They seem to defy the appropriate laws of architecture and physics that gather around plant physiology (physiognomy?), too big, too weighty, too fraught with glamour and purposelessness.

But what do I know about plant purposes and botany? I just want to raise the dahlias for your delectation or have people look like them. I watched pollinating bees on PBS last night get sucked into the throats of giant protea to do their replicating duty. What it might look like to zero in on the nub of a giant dahlia with its petticoats raised I can barely imagine. I lean in anyway in my human way and sniff: next to nothing, but not nothing. The hint of hay that chrysanthemums give off. A light broth of cellulose and sun.

⊡   ⊡   ⊡

It's fun, even a challenge, but inaccurate. A dahlia is only like itself, and children can't be flowers. Language is impoverished, a wild bouquet of tangents and mistakes. We push it and pull it, are pushed and pulled. Come close; just miss; no bulls eye; humbled by the limitlessness of comparison, the never-ending parsing of perceptual nuance. David, in the second grade, was ardently spinning similes; he had the sense of mission and a deep sensuality but not the properties of equation. The metaphoric impulse sprayed loosely: "His ears look like two little lovely moon. His nose look like a boat. His mouth look like a water."

[I'd tried the figuration exercise years before on a group of recalcitrant high school holdbacks, in summer school to make up lost English time. Suffering and ill-used by the system, they had little patience for my honky Shakespeare lesson, with its Shakespeare sonnet fulcrum: "'The eye of heaven,' so, we could say, 'The sun is like. . . .' What is the sun like? Or, for example, 'It's as hot as . . .'

Monique, it's as hot as . . . what?"

Slouching, "I dunno." Rolls her eyes.

"But think about it . . . The sun is like an eye. It's as hot as . . ."

Shrugs. "I dunno . . . It's as hot as fuck!"]

Little David had things more under control, but there was in him a primal explosion of meanings that hadn't yet narrowed itself to live singularly in a leaf or one face. You either have to have a word for exactly every element and thought—not going to happen—or you let things be in and of their nature and attend them. Or you just take out your pen (or Powerbook) and run through the fields in a hopeless happy rush calling, "like a lion's mane," "like a French chanteuse in a spotlight" (this dahlia was ruffled white, with thin red piping out of Chanel), or "my nipples are such peonies" (Bob Glück), or "these swollen roses puffed on the dining room table, creaming pale magenta, lavender and pink in a moiré pattern, fading color into color the way silk does, seizing light and inhabiting the shine from within" (me, in *Unbound,* really pushing it.)

The great still life painters, you know, painting before photography and presaging its duty, caught the verisimilitude of plants and flowers in much the same way portrait painters did humans, but with this difference: Their richest challenge was to assemble one of those giant bouquets in a way that *couldn't* exist in real life, a full year's range of blooms present, each of which would have died in its season before the others began to bud. The impossible flowers held together this side of being "like" Nature. They were *made*.

"The big sky does art in the river," wrote second-grader Carlesia, in full possession of a gift for iconic imagery. Tamisha, from the rather worldlier fourth, saw things more literally, but with an urge toward utopia clarifying her intent. Printing carefully on wide-ruled paper, she conjured for her readers "the really world," where, she explained with determination, "they can say what they really mean."

READING IN TIME, READING IN PLACE

As if you could simply square space (you're in the center on a chaise longue, or favorite living-room armchair, or clean spot of green lawn) and then superimpose upon this newly bounded zone the page you are holding: a text fixed in the time and place of its reading. Today's placid air has the supple, smooth texture of warm water, a tactile, surrounding softness for my act of projective geometry, reading *Don Quixote* on just such a blue chaise longue inside a slip of wisteria shade at the edge of a borrowed summerhouse in the wilderness hills of Northern California, nailing it to the scene.

I learned some years ago that a deep physical context—exotic locale or familiar, invested terrain—often asks for a deep book; the union of conflated intensities will become unbreakable. I'd been couched, then, on the southern shores of Crete—long, slow, fiery August days of limitless horizon across the Libyan Sea. The water *exactly* swimmable, the stretch of sea and sand and sky one entirety, a unified gleam—and so deeply saturating that you *were* the scene you looked at.

Slung back in a plastic chair at a waterfront café I pored over Proust—a second summer's immersion—as far from urbane Paris as you could get and yet wholly assimilated into the verbal stream, Frenchified. I read contentedly for hours, devoured by sentences as long as the long horizon. At a clausal pitch I glanced up from St. Germain des Prés to notice the frontal, shimmering waves: singular Greek generosity. How could I lose myself in a book in *this* unimaginable spot, a place so sensuously present as to be—as it would soon become—iconic, soul's body warm in Paradise? The body of Proust's text was up to the challenge. I read down and looked up, read down and looked up—exactly the same! Fullness and particularity, vista and grain; each way my investment was total, at each cast I was invited in to partake of totality. The arranged marriage would speak together in two languages forever.

Now July has given way to the rueful, exuberant Spanish knight annealed to a contemplative vista of royal palm, redwood, California bay and—did I say?—swimming pool. It will never have taken place any other way. Every morning I've followed the shade from deck, to bower, to green tile, reading up and down into the superimposed frames, laughing out loud, exhilarated on vacation and howlingly . . . Cervantified. "How long do you have this house for?" "A full month." "Wow." "What are you reading?" "*Don Quixote*; a new translation." "The whole thing?" "950 pages!" "Wow!" The interpenetration has been extravagant.

And yet, with ten long summer days to go, I've finished the book. A scramble into other, slighter, realms proves fruitless; the book needs to be as commanding as this rented pleasure palace. I remember a title long on my backlist: *The Road to Xanadu*, a study of my beloved Coleridge by John Lowes. This must be its time! I curve downhill past towering Mt. Tamalpais, past madrones in their burgundy nudity and sleek houses cantilevered across the valley, to the woodsy library of Fairfax where I find, listed on the computer, one county copy in the nearby town of San Rafael.

The next morning I'm there, searching the indicated shelf . . . Coleridge: poems, prose, biography, *The Way to Xanadu* . . . [Way? That's not right; it's supposed to be a road!] by . . . Caroline Alexander.

"Excuse me. Thanks. I'm looking for *The Road to Xanadu*. I checked on the computer yesterday and it said you had one copy on the shelf."

The librarian jumps right to my side, happy to have a customer lost in the ultra-literary aisle, where she may now swim. She pulls out *The Way* . . . and presents it to me kindly. I explain the difference and she returns to her desk to study the conundrum. Down in a squat I examine the nearby rows: Byron . . . Chaucer . . . Chesterton; Dryden on the other side; Coleridge, Coleridge, Coleridge, but no *Road*.

"Here it is!" the librarian calls from the information

desk, waving an old green hardback. Startled, I amble over warily. Embossed in gold: *The Road to Xanadu: A Study in the Ways of the Imagination* by John Livingston Lowes.

Chagrined, she motions to a shelf below. "It was here waiting to be tossed out. The other librarian was going through the shelves just an hour ago and pulled it; it hasn't been checked out for years, and we needed the room."

Slightly sheepish, she's nevertheless gracious; I'm practically levitating. I've well known that you find books at the right time, and even that books find you, but such a fortuitous simultaneous adoption has never before taken place. If I'd arrived an hour later it would probably have been down the chute. I proudly accept custody, and drive home with *The Road to Xanadu* strapped to the passenger seat.

When a book works the world coheres. July draws to an end with this astonishing study of Coleridge's sources as he began to write "The Rime of the Ancient Mariner" and "Kubla Khan;" an intrepid reading of an indefatigable reader and what he was reading before he was writing; a radial contemplation of adventure writers, naturalists, voyages of discovery, and biblical or mythic tales that feed the poetry; a work that may stand, as others have suggested, as the first real hypertext, nexus of concurrent lines of information and linkage. We see alligators, icebergs, fierce north winds, geysering streams, spliced into the emerging poems as a live process of interactive collage. The bristling document fills my hands, necessary anchor; the warm air settles. At peace in little Xanadu, then, I read of big Xanadu, and the vision of the vision of the vision brings me through summer's closing days.

For days I repeat this tale of timely discovery to a number of friends; several finish my telling with "and so they gave you the book." It would never have occurred to me to ask, but at week's end I give the library a call. "Well, we hadn't really *decided* to de-access it; it was under consideration."

"If you *are* going to get rid of it," I suggest diplomatically, "I'd certainly love to have it." I imagine paying any reasonable used-book price. In the late afternoon when the breeze picks up, strumming the tall bamboo and driving turkey vultures into smoother and smoother arcs, there's a message on the rented home's machine: "If you'd like to come by we will be pleased to give you our copy of *The Road to Xanadu.*"

⊞   ⊞   ⊞

A long time ago, when I was a quite young man, I began to read Proust in earnest for the first time. I can see the place—a small attic room in Cambridge, Mass., and a correspondingly small park below—and I can see the printed scene—Marcel, the narrator, equally young, watches the glorious courtesan Odette while she rides through the Bois de Boulogne, "borne along by the flight of a pair of fiery horses, . . . on her lips an ambiguous smile in which I read only the benign condescension of majesty." It took me seventeen years to turn that first foray into a fluid reading that led me through all seven volumes in a couple of summers, in Paris, and in Crete, and finally home in San Francisco.

At book's end, when Marcel, much older, encounters Odette at a party, much older, powdered and painted and just recognizable by virtue of being so, he remembers when he first saw her, many years before, when she ruled the Bois de Boulogne of his youthful imagination. From the comfort of my San Francisco sofa, as he conjured her early image, I remembered when *I* first saw her, similarly almost a lifetime ago, when he was young and *I* was young, and Odette made us hold our breath together in the *Allée des Acacias*, as she "cast, almost imperceptibly, a sweeping glance round her." I saw, too, my faraway attic rooms in Cambridge (where fervent R, in the middle of the night, shook the whole building I thought was falling down, climbing up the fire escape to surprise me in bed), and then the small cobblestone square where I sat on a bench with a precious book in my hands that opened onto Paris, in which a scandalous woman in lilac veils (however re-gendered) stole the heart of a neurasthenic young man, who memorized her form. I read across my years of his years—Paris, Combray, Cambridge, Crete, San Francisco—as the simultaneous frames, aging together, were united: How many times and locales had conspired to engage the powers by which I experienced the magic transposition of actually having participated in the long, inclusive life of the book!

I lean, now, on the narrator's shoulder to imagine: a scented grove of acacias in powdery, yellow bloom. Odette de Crécy, the celebrated Mme Swann, "this woman whose reputation for beauty, misconduct, and elegance was universal," absolutely eager with eros and alert to all possibilities, casts her famous wandering glance around the scripted park, narrows into momentary focus, and finds *me.*

Susan comes over—she's the *best* audience—her genius is receptivity—to see my refinished (rent-controlled) apartment for the first time.

"Oh my god . . . ," she's histrionic exactly as you would wish. I'm excited like a child with a new toy (a big new toy), showing off the handiwork (mostly executed by others) as well as my executive direction of the redone scene, and the positioned objects that charge its newly burnished space. "The floor . . . !"

"Isn't it beautiful?" I crow. I restrain myself from pushing her down to feel the skin of the polished wood.

"Yes! It's *so* bright."

We drink in the space. "I know! Everyone said don't do natural pine, it'll wind up looking like the Adirondacks—but it's perfect, isn't it?"

"Oh my god . . ."

Susan tours the apartment, noticing everything I've done to be noticed: the mottling of the red-tinged caramel floor (tip of the hat to Mr. Ha and his crew of speedy elves), the new paint job (Antiquated White and Siberian Iris—I'm so queer I'm happy just to be able to *say* Siberian Iris!), the surprisingly under-decorated walls, the vases, the vases, all the cherished items in their specified array; the vases.

"It really makes a difference, doesn't it?"

"Oh . . . god . . . I'm so jealous."

"What do you mean?—your house is beautiful." It's a sweet Berkeley bungalow with a garden and a half.

"I know, I love it," she says hugging herself, "but it always moves me when other people personalize their spaces."

Susan is a therapist; she has projective empathy. When she says "jealous" she means she's ready to love what you love and defend it. Her generous delectation is professionally and constitutionally conspiratorial: She wants people to believe in themselves.

Sharpening her gaze she charts the apartment item by item, just as I have done: the arrangements and their constituent parts, ascensions, declensions, counterpoise, and arcs. I show her the new giant vase—consort to a queen—with its green-brushed yellow glaze that seems to melt down the octagonal sides like ice cream. It's very heavy; I place it in her hands, turn it like a cosmos. This piece partners a more rounded, voluminous version on the other side of the room, echo and amplitude. The cool thick glaze has the elemental feel of rock. A golden weighted column to hold up nothing but delicate flowers, pulsating obelisk of saturated color, my monolith. "See?"

"Oh my god . . ."

Night after night in my middle-aged life I stay at home and watch my apartment, mirror of my desiring self. Susan with her magnanimous way and discriminating eye has recognized the intensity of my engagement, how each picture on the wall, each crafted thing, is not merely beautiful but *matters.* She nods her head to my relentless prompts and clarifies. "Yes," she says, "they resonate. Maybe it's not what I would do or choose, but it's all yours. I love that. It's *you.*"

On my sofa [hardwood frame, eight-way hand-tied springs, down-wrapped cushions—the story behind it was buy a sofa to last a lifetime, led by my friends with AIDS whose first final purchases were always couches to be comfortable dying on] I look at the living room spread like a performance before me. It's a glowing set of active correspondence and magic placement, utterly, ceaselessly composed (I'm the guy who can't write at my desk unless the bed is made). I could say I direct myself in this theater of the self but I could also say I act myself, frames within frames of shifting personhood.

The beaming floor melds with Japanese small cabinets and mid-century modern tables: clean lines that meditate on balance and wood-glow. Noguchi paper lamp shaped like a condom ready to blast off into space; hand-beaten copper bowl from Santa Clara del Cobre in Michoacán, where I watched the artist fire and pull and pound the radiant metal; a porcelain Chinese lady in polished detail reading a book but stepping in clouds, so for me she's a muse—oh, an inventory fails the task, and maybe only I can decipher the complexities. The room is like a poem where every element is in conversation with every other—a poetics of decoration, then, by which I bring my lazy self once again to attention, *placed*.

There's the modest dementia, here, of one who's lived alone too long. There's the queen partaking of a totally estheticized environment. There's the scholar surrounded by books and shelves and mythic objects with Romantic pedigrees. There's the artist in love with creative order, and the poet obsessed with the meaning of parts. The place throbs like an organism: a *living* room!

Susan stays for tea as the light falls. I point out how evening deepens the orange in the floor, settles the room. We're both exhausted from so much appreciation. I light the lamps, upping the amber, lengthening the rays from everything yellow or gold. Sure, as I've gotten older the items have gotten a bit pricier, but I did the same when I had a pasteboard dresser and hand-me-down pots. You *make* a home, and you fill a space with the coordinates of an inner composition.

I'm smaller when Susan leaves, but my rooms stay large, with their drama of intention and desperate specificity. I close the drapes and lower the blinds, a corner of blue-gray squares. Perfect solitude.

ABATTOIR
A Diptych

At the faculty reading last night Karl read a wicked, spot-on piece about a guy searching the city for a guy he'd met by chance, who electrified him erotically, invaded his fantasies, and preoccupied his strategic waking life— a guy high on his List of Favorite Eligible Men, who haunt the peripheries of any single San Francisco gay man's social circuit, and who engender a benign kind of stalking as determined bachelors fish each other's faces for the hooks in each other's eyes.

Then Rob stepped up to the mike with his earnest black oversized glasses and enunciatory poetic style, and read fiercely from a long work with intense language specificity, alternately caressing and spitting a dramatic lexicon that included the word "abattoir."

I ran with the sound and the spit and the sense— *abattoir*—right to my adolescent years in Texas, where I'd arrived upended at the age of nine from my midtown Manhattan upbringing, touching down in flatland oil-rigged East Texas racist deep-South Yankee-hating bug-infested small town otherness. We were driving on the outskirts of Ft. Worth—a very Western-seeming cattle town then—stockyards and rail yards and slaughterhouses the only punctuation marks—when we passed a roadside sign declaiming proudly, "Fresh Killed Meat." As fast as an involuntary contraction my brother shouted, "Quick! Stop the car!" as he plunged headlong out the door of the Chevrolet to vomit up his tender New York City insides.

Abattoir: I ran with the spit and the spit and the sense in and out of our furnished suburban Texas house—not just other people's furniture but other people's *things*—in and out of the moonscape lakes filled with tangled driftwood, under the stark pine shadows and over the crusty pine-needle mounds, by the pitch-black outside wall of the Longview Hilton which proved to be a 50-foot-high solid mass of twitching crickets, through the Jewishness of my Yankeeness—*abattoir*—to land on our front lawn circa 1956 by the great pecan tree with its green big-toe nuts, for a celebratory occasion—Christmas? my birthday?—must have been that, because my neighborhood friend Jimmy had given me a present. With his spiky crew cut, freckled upturned nose, and bright red cheeks he could have been a puppet boy—Pinocchio or Howdy Doody—but he possessed a dark, mischievous turn that was more like a mean streak—*abattoir*—and though we played frequently he was way too much a boy's boy for my natural comfort. He'd handed me an oblong box casually wrapped in tissue paper. This was the era of plastic models you glued together—I'd made everything from jet planes to Model Ts to aircraft carriers to missile silos—so I was happy enough to be getting one more.

I opened the box: "Wha . . . ? Oh." I held in my hands a group of tiny green and brown plastic toy soldiers—I wasn't even sure at first what they were *for*—which I thought right then was some battalion of his rejects—they were clearly used—a mismatched set of over-killed infantrymen with battle fatigue at best. "Umm, thanks." I might as well have been clutching a box of dead crickets. What could I do with these hapless veterans? I had *no* interest in staging military maneuvers or having my little men shoot and maim each other, and I thought Jimmy probably knew that: He had on one of his smirks that suggested "Sucker!" The gift had none of the almost libidinal spark new toys have; it was pointless. (If I had, in fact, already assembled armadas of technological armaments, those were seen as puzzles—intricate, working machines to piece together like my beloved Erector Set—not as war implements.)

I stood in the yard with my box of inert beings who'd been slaughtered so many times they could have no blood left, and silently cursed Jimmy's freckled normalcy, and bitterly reproached his dead-ass fantasies, his crass stinginess, and quietly slipped into a growing, marooned panic as the unforgiving Texas sun split the pecans on their branches, rotted the still-rounding pears, and dried to a trickle the last rusty water at the colored-only drinking fountain I'd seen downtown. I stood lost in the heat of our open lawn as if in the full expanse of an old lost prairie—of the Great Plains itself—where my beloved skyscrapers were tumbleweeds now, shredding the farther and still-farther horizon . . .

▫ ▫ ▫

This afternoon I ran into Karl at a gay neighborhood café where he sat by the sunlit window squintingly grading papers.

"That was a great reading last night," I said, "pitch perfect."

"Thanks," he answered genuinely. "I was happy with the response. You never know."

"It worked completely; people loved it." He then admitted he'd been worried that an unsympathetic character was portrayed too sympathetically.

"Well, it wasn't so much the character as the snappy things he said. What was that great line when the stranger he'd seen at the bar showed up completely by chance at the park?"

"'I thought you'd never get here.'"

"Yeah, perfect." I made a quick arc with my head to scan the café and shuffled my feet. Window sun heated the wooden benches where the boys in T-shirts pored over bitter coffee and notebook computers.

"Here grading papers too?" Karl asked.

"Actually," I confessed, "I'm doing what your character did: I'm 'looking' for someone."

"One of your 'favorites'?"

"Number one," I sighed (there was only one) and completed my scan to confirm that he wasn't there. "Back to the other café," I shrugged.

"Good luck!"

I bowed out the door and slinked up the street where another café waited. Just yesterday morning I'd spotted a man there cast to my absolute preference—studying at a table across from mine—who smiled at me discreetly, and then not discreetly. He left before any assignation was possible, but not before firing my fantasies into life from the old slaughterhouse floor, and raising to compulsion my determination to track this fellow down and match his lovely heartbeat to mine. *"I thought you'd never get here."*

So this morning I'd gone to that café at the same hour, under cover of washing my sheets at the laundromat across the street, peering intently at the back of every black-haired stranger and surveying the sidewalks where every toy soldier marching was identically *not* him.

"OK," I thought, "I'll *make* him come out," believing for the moment in that coercive astral power the science of lust pretends to. I went to the Museum of Modern Art expecting to run into him—just me and him in the big city—and I didn't, then stopped back at the café just in case, but there *was* no case—sliding on to a second café down the street where I was now sure I'd seen him once before and in which, among the laptop crowd whose circumspect cruising eyes just cleared the tops of their laptops, Karl sat reviewing student stories, having already written—having publicly read!—the perfected version of my own obsessive narrative line.

Later in the evening, after a movie, still possessed by a hopelessly hopeful restlessness, out on the darkened sex-slick streets of the Castro—the Cat's Row, I call it— where I *never* prowl—*abattoir*—I downed an acrid beer in the darkest of the too-dark bars, and passed once more by the original café now lit up as if with revelers, filling out my activated pattern whose purpose was entirely liminal—sex? marriage?—but whose structure seemed inviolable as I followed my empty urgings to their illogical conclusions, assaulted by happenstance— a stranger at a table—on the pooling floor of this slaughterhouse of desire, that was relentlessly of my construction and constructed me.

Steered by an almost planetary force I'd sleepwalked from café to café to museum to café to café to bar to café. By the end of the weary evening, as I trudged to my car, his face began to blur from repeated conjuring—then I willed it into concretion. It burns in this night sky, shedding no light, *way* out of reach of the street it will not illumine . . .

THE DANCERS

I'm a homophile, a bibliophile, a litterateur, an opera buff, a cinemaphile and foreign film fanatic, a gourmand and on a good day a gourmet; I'm a closet soprano; I have piano envy at least an octave long; I'm an art aficionado, really a frustrated painter, and ultimately a Rembrandt whore; I'm a Grecophile, a Francophile, a Proustophile, and a Chopiniste, an esthete, a sensualist, a sybarite, a voluptuary, or a slut; I'm a slave to "Animal Planet," a wildflower stalker, an orchid addict, a blissed-out gardener and an unrepentant vase queen . . . but in truth I've never really been a balletomane—until, that is, I saw the Kirov Ballet of the Mariinsky Theatre perform Balanchine's *Jewels* on a Saturday night in October.

I know less about pas de chats than pussycats. There were signs, though, it could have gone a different way, that a natural inclination might have developed, beyond ballet's easy, morphic lure of butt, thigh, and extended neck. There's the issue of Tchaikovsky, for example, on crackly 78s of *Swan Lake*, soundtrack behind the giggles of my brother and me as we turned and leapt, arms aflutter, twinkling along the sweeping curve of our living room sofa just where it edged the round glass coffee table, me imitating him imitating some image of feminine grace visible even to an eight-year-old—as always his fruity leanings cast at a riskier angle than mine—but older imitation swan and younger nevertheless dancing together in a trailing pas de deux worthy of ducklings, at least, crossing to the other side of the road. The sweeping Romantic score was punctuated by squeals; think of tickling your nephew, approaching with fingers outspread as his shrieks of delight increase, fingers closing in upon open nerves: the high giggles of helpless abandon, of limitless imagination, of sprung glee. The curl of the sofa encouraged our giddy line of pirouette and skip, but it was decades before I realized the circular glass table *was* Swan Lake as we danced, possessed, around its moonlit shore. (And it was ten years before ballet-student Kathy demonstrated for us the actual tripping cygnet steps, with their high mince and low lifts, their crossed hands from children's games and the alarming, yearned-for unison of their head flips and kicklets.)

But that was just tomfoolery—or *hen*foolery; for each of us the impulse toward refinement went in other directions, the ardor of pursuit attaching itself to other worthy systems. Sure I'd seen Nureyev and Fonteyn in their heyday, and productions of the moribund story ballets in greater or smaller grandeur, but as I grew older much of the pleasure waned: How could that fusty manner and seamless, aristocratic unnaturalism hold my focus, whose own poetic lyricism was now tempered by slippage and fracture, the indeterminate edges of surrender? I watched and didn't swoon; I leapt and fell.

But because we are culture mavens together and because I trust his lead, I followed my old friend Gene to Berkeley where a rare visit by the newly coined Kirov Ballet of the Mariinsky Theatre (formerly Leningrad Kirov) would bring its masterly, arcane sensibility to bear upon Balanchine's *Jewels*, the first full-length non-narrative ballet ever choreographed (1967).

I approached Zellerbach Hall under the wing of Gene's full-spread anticipation; it's rare that I, an acknowledged Swan King, revert to cygnet steps, but in matters of opera and dance I defer to Gene, his informed specificity, his seen-everything history and his systematic memory of performer and place. "Don't miss it," he'd urged—but I had no particular expectation. Certainly I was up for a public event in my fetching new aqua rayon shirt, in my new teal sportcoat with its plush, touch-me-please sheen. Zellerbach at intermission could be an excellent place to cruise. (Oh, come on, *any* dance performance is an excellent place to cruise!) [I'm a homophile, a sensualist, a voluptuary, etc.]

Jewels is set in three refractions: emeralds, rubies, and diamonds; at the center of each is a ballerina *in excelsis*; green, red, or silver-white inflame the stage, the lights, the costumes, brilliant in monochrome; the whole ballet unified only by this rush of color, the intensity of spectral light dancing from a jewel. "Emeralds" that night, as I remember, was fine; it was green; it was unremarkable; it was ballet. The ballerina struck sparks but failed to ignite. I didn't really feel my body stretch in sympathy; I didn't want to *be* her. I settled in for an evening like an evening.

There's a Turgenev story I know well—"The Singers," from his *Sportsman's Notebook*—which features a tavern in the village of Kolotovka high on the Russian steppes. Yasha the Turk and a traveling salesman compete for a quart of beer in a singing contest. Up first, the salesman reels out a high falsetto and proceeds with embellishments and decorative passages worthy of a coloratura, with "such flourishes, such tongue-clickings and drummings, such wild throat-play" the acclaim is instantaneous and complete: "Congratulations—the quart is yours!" says Muddlehead. "Yasha can't touch you."

As the curtain went up on "Rubies," the crimson enthusiasm of Stravinsky's capriccio was in full flame, and Irina Golub, my program says, eyeballed me with red spears that kicked my own flints into fires, precocious and ferocious, an ingénue in complete control of seduction and desire. She seemed tiny; she was possessed by joy; she was flirting with the audience with such specific abandon that I felt sure each and every ballet goer was convinced she was looking at them—in fact, I'm convinced she did look every single person in the eye, and that was her gift. She was totally on view, totally available, full-tilt in love with performing and anyone who would be her knowing audience. She lived in transference. She couldn't stop laughing and leaping. Her scarlet ecstasy spurted across the stage, showered the audience who couldn't release from the eye lock, the lip lock, the embrace. Clearly she'd be the Kirov's new star, and she was showing us her youthful stuff, serving notice to the old guard of prima ballerinas. She had every edge and glint of ruby light at her command. This, I thought in a rush (she *made* me think) is exactly what performing has to be: the generosity, the willful dialectic, the endless acknowledgment of shared meaning or joy. It was a demonstration of how to make art—the outward-seeking contract, the *givingness* at the heart of creation. In extension, in leap, in dizzyless twirl she watched us watching her: art's mediation of knowledge and intuition. She was a munificent tease, a harlot of promise, alive entirely in the transitive act. She was transaction incarnate; incarnadine.

I stumbled into intermission in something like exhaustion, tingling. Now I knew why I was there. ["Now in a moment I know what I am for"—Whitman—"and already a thousand singers, a thousand songs . . . have started to life within me."] Out in the lobby Gene and I crowed in mutual admiration as we surveyed the scintillated crowd, devotees, now, of "Rubies," of *Irina.* The buzz was audible and visible; pink had collectively infused cheek and brow. We thumbed through the program to verify our wonder, and chart the excitement to come.

In "The Singers," after a lot of prodding, Yasha the Turk does take the stage, eyes barely visible under lowered lashes. His first note seems to come "not from his chest, but from somewhere far way, as if it had chanced to fly into the room." Within seconds Yasha's mournful tune has pierced the hearts of his listeners; "with every note there floated out something noble and immeasurably large, like familiar steppe country unfolding before you, stretching away into the boundless distance." "With the scarcely perceptible inner quivering of passion, which pierces like an arrow" Yasha finds the measure of the Russian soul, and—victorious—leaves his listeners slumped in tears over their beers.

Part Three of *Jewels* draws in master Tchaikovsky to set a rousing old-world stage for "Diamonds" (his symphony No. 3 composed just before *Swan Lake*): It's ballet as imperial ballet. There was pure, neutral, diamond-light now, crystalline sobriety, clarity of purpose. High noon or full moon. Uliana Lopatkina, a Kirov veteran, wound herself in this shining stream, a cone of radiance sheathing her. She advanced with the authority of necessity, her eyes almost blank, because they were two points on a traveling body, not beacons leading it. Frozen in white light, burning in white light, a hush surrounding every step, she was a sleepwalker, clairvoyant, a space walker, striding or gliding into new stratospheres of axis and tilt. She bounded into the air, pausing impossibly to shimmer at the apex of her arc; she stood still and *shed* glitter. Every place she stepped was the center of a new circle, and only the center. She made no acknowledgement of the audience, the stage, even of the other dancers. If she saw *anything* I didn't see her see. Solemn purpose closed her off and revealed her, spun into a vortex that was a living, transparent cocoon of moving focus. She had security and dynamism fused in such a way that all registrations of finesse were marked inwardly; she saw *inside* the dance. Unmarred by smiles or glances, she breathed into each extension, into the formation of line and lift, as if the music impelled her to be that way. Her control was absolute, but it was determined by her fierce yielding to the science of gravity; to the geometry of circles, arcs, and complete perpendicular extension; to the higher mathematics of harmony; the spiritual order of melody; the organic chemistry of limb, torso, digit living their limits. She couldn't tease or seduce or reward because she knew she had no claim on "Diamonds"; by virtue of devotion she'd become a clear refractor herself, flashing out from a central negation all light that came in.

Uliana Lopatkina danced for me that night with full pedagogic intensity, to instill in me unwaveringly the means by which practice supersedes intention, emotional intensity has core containment, and personal completion may be read, ultimately, as not being yourself at all. Silence was her measure and mark; attention made her beautiful; rigor became her ecstasy; control set free abundance and elation. She performed some utter stillness at the heart of movement, centripetal, a magnet, a sun. By virtue of the matrix she generated we were pulled into orbit, supercharged particles: her audience. Together we witnessed—she did and we did—an examination of balance that erased boundaries and redrew them to include the whole stage, the audience, her partners, the corps de ballet, because her focus held that long and that far and that hard: diamond significance. I didn't want to be her. I wanted to be her dance.

Sometimes laughter is the only appropriate expression of awe, and we laughed our way out of the hall that night, shaking our heads, light on our feet, transported. How does the curtain close on such a narrative of *Jewels?* How did we get home, go to sleep, become discrete units? How unclasp the precious stones, lay them aside? Without a dance vocabulary I had only metaphor to aid me, and the felt immediacy of description, and my own yearning for structural coherence, a dream of form. Within a week I'd brought *Jewels* into the writing classroom, hoping to transfer the terms.

"I turned away and struck off quickly down the hill on which Kolotovka stands," Turgenev tells us at the end of "The Singers," surrounded by "the misty waves of evening haze." He hears a child's name called out in the darkness, "Antropka-a-a," echoing in air "full of the shadows of night." Turgenev, the village of Kolotovka, Stravinsky, Tchaikovsky, Balanchine, Golub, Lupatkina, Antropka-a-a: Might I dare to claim my Russian forebears—*Shurin from Dniepropetrovsk*—and read into this closing scene a shadow of my own, a small boy dancing around a glassy lake in which he catches, for the first time, the fullness of his reflection? Mists part to reveal a moon of spotlight clarity (or a table lamp by the sofa); its white beam proposes for us the delicate arch of his back, his youthful attempt at extension, the swanlike lift of his pint-size port-de-bras, his truly visionary skips, the ease with which he can make himself twizzle and twirl in the air . . . even while giggling.

AVATAR

> If a man could pass through Paradise in a
> dream, and have a flower presented to him
> as a pledge that his soul had really been
> there, and if he found that flower in his
> hand when he woke—Ay! And what then?
>
> —COLERIDGE

Nobody wants to hear someone else's dream: the flat factuality outside of proof, the seemingly arbitrary twists and turns, the locked symbolism, the reverent silliness. Heads nod, eyes roll up; the dream recounter unravels obliviously, being self-entranced narrator, subject, characters, event, coder, and decoder all at once: a narcissist in paradise.

Nevertheless we all recklessly dare the odds, and because she is curious and because she is curiously awake to language, I tell Tavi, my co-worker, about my new dream, or as much of it as I can remember the following day. The Creative Writing Program office holds these conversations tenderly: Image making and narrative frames are part of its regular procedures. Half-drawn blinds block out the over-determining sun,

125

lending the still, warm, room an air of quiet expectation, and letting dream figures bleed into the shadows.

"I was killed by the Nazis," I begin with a matter-of-fact punch. "I was part of a theater troupe; they came into the auditorium with machine guns and fired at us in the lobby. I almost got away, but I didn't. I was shot and killed."

Tavi looks at me with focused but expressionless eyes, patiently waiting for the inevitable plot permutations.

"That's it," I say, shrugging. "I died." Pause for effect. "But I didn't disappear. I died, but never lost consciousness. I stayed with it."

"You mean you didn't really die?"

"No, I died. But I was able to maintain some kind of awareness through the process. It didn't really hurt, and it wasn't *that* difficult. I knew I had to concentrate, but I knew how to do it. I just stayed centered, stayed conscious. I sort of narrowed into myself. Things were transpiring outside of me, but I remained concentrated, contained. Time passed, and then I realized I'd become someone new.

"That's the whole dream: I was shot, I died, I stayed conscious, I was someone else."

"At the end," Tavi threads a needle, "were you a baby?"

"No, not really. I went through a transition, and

then at some point I realized what had happened—I don't know how much time it took—and I was another person."

Tavi's gathered the eerie details, and considers carefully. We look at each other, in the saddle of an inconclusive narrative searching for resolution. The tension has us high in the seat, leaning into momentum.

"Were you . . . *you?*"

"Yeah, I guess so—I think I was—I was myself *now.*" Her line of questioning begins to suggest something new: I'd taken the dream as a kind of parable, an intrigue of classic, symbolic action, but if, in the end, I stood as "myself" now, could the dream, in fact, be seen as a backwards account, a view into a past life, the immediate prelude to my present incarnation? I shiver at this unanticipated thought, and Tavi, who jostles for verbal place in a program too full of writers, is proud to have given me the shivers.

"But here's my question," I continue. "At the waking point, coming into language, I asked myself, 'What do we call the person who stays conscious through reincarnation? Buddha?'—but I knew that wasn't it. As I searched my vocabulary coming out of the dream I seized on the word, 'avatar.' But I'm not sure that's right either."

Tavi's signed on to be the co-conspirator of my dream, alive to tangents as she always is, to the small divagations in any conversation that might point to something unexpected: a terrier of talk. We look up "avatar" in the dictionary and it's true, it isn't exactly appropriate (the Hindu term for a deity's earthly manifestation: much too grand) and neither is "Bodhisattva" or anything else I can come up with. Besides, I don't actually believe in reincarnation, have no Buddhist training and little natural Buddhist sympathy. In any case, I've always thought the purpose of incarnation would be to revel in the body, not to drop it. I'm a Romantic in the Keatsian mode: The difficult interaction with matter makes your soul dimensional, authenticates it. You are *in* life to relish the embodiment, and if it's just a sensory dance— then *love* the illusion! Isn't the body made precisely for engaging materiality, not transcending it?

I don't ask these questions in the office, though they remain underneath the itchy, heated surface of my dream, a vocabulary posed and a lexicon suspended. We table the investigation for now, with a charge hanging in the small, bureaucratic room, the nervous scent of unfinished business recast by the pride of dogged pursuit. The chase, after all, has awakened us, sleek and twitching after the hunt.

A few days later at the Zuni café, over a sumptuously incarnate lunch, I recount the dream to Diane, who is, indeed, a Buddhist, a determined and informed one. We've been placed fraternally side-by-side along an adobe wall, with the brick oven before us, hush of fire, circle of warmth. To my working ideas of past-life revelation and traditional, coded symbolism, Diane adds the concept of "rehearsal." "That's very good," she says instructionally. "You're *practicing.*"

The ground shifts suddenly towards the future from the past—where *is* the center of this dream?—and I shift with it: a mortal augury, now? Spooked, I activate my peripheral vision to look for the shadowy swing of a scythe nearby—then spoon a dollop of butterscotch pot de crème to soothe the panic. "Do you know what the word is for the person who stays awake through reincarnation?" I ask, hoping for some concretion. "It's not 'avatar,' is it?"

"I don't think so, I'm not sure, but I'll check. And you know, the word Buddhists use for that consciousness which goes through multiple lives is 'mindstream.' Isn't that nice? We would say you were in mindstream."

The word *is* lovely, and I meditate on the implications for several days. How did I, the earthbound, the sensualist, the image-maker, know how to remain in mindstream, or even what it was, or how it felt? I'd certainly never thought about it beforehand; what did I actually *do* in my stream? "It was similar to compositional mind," I explain to another friend pressed into service as a dream-audience, "where you lock intensely onto writing while the whole world swirls through."

Everything you know and see is there but you abide in a kind of determined surrender, deepened into focus, yourself and not yourself.

Yourself—then also, your *self.* Apparently, in the dream, I wasn't afraid to die because I knew how to be steady in sight of the next my-body; I was perfectly secure in the happy fact that I'd *get* to reincarnate. Was I bound, then, to the wheel of living like a lover? Three weeks later I can still will myself to feel what it was like to be inside of mindstream, hunkered down to an elemental purpose, riding the various storm, the waves, some cosmic wind, a tunneling chain of changes, until I emerge myself again, *out* of mindstream but *into* body, this body having dreamed itself a new body, trained and familiar and wakeful and enlarged.

For assurance I check my Webster one last time: a second, smaller, definition, hidden among the "avatar" citations, "an incarnation or embodiment of another *person*"—so not a deity invoked but . . . the avatar of *myself*? It had been, in fact, a dark and derelict winter. But a narrow passage outside of time and space squeezed me along its walls like a boa constrictor and pushed me through. If I *have* somehow managed to give birth to me (again), who then, body in hand, might I become this time, and how in this world will I get there?

IN THE BARS OF HEAVEN AND HELL

> O, damn these things that try to maim me
> This armor
> Fooled
> Alive in its
> Self
>
> —JACK SPICER

> In time Cupid himself, healed of his wound,
> escapes . . . and joins Psyche. . . . and Love
> may thus be said to have rescued the mind.
>
> —W. JACKSON BATE

A series of false starts, holes, memory in junk mode, flashing signs that won't hold, missing letters: *wet pain* for *wet paint, urn* for *turn, trance* for *entrance* . . .

A sequence of overtures, preludes, entryways leading to the same core, a hub of alleys in the heart of the underground city, San Francisco of bright men in dreamtime and lost boys all me, 1965–69, who will become a civic stalwart and one of the seen-it-alls, furious partisan within ten short years, for forty years and more . . . Imaginary metropolis, *fleur de ciel,* balm for a wound and the wound's own inflamer, city of promise or pleasure or pain, city of the heathenly heavenly gate, city of all gratification given or lost in place, still there, still here, still there . . .

A net into which I am pushing myself falling, talking to origin, walking home, walking away, counting backwards: 58, 47, 36, 29, 18! December 1965 when the siren began to wail, the house shake from its foundation, the wildflower open that wouldn't close, perfuming the small rooms, the glittering streets, the lowering classrooms and lecture halls, infusing the bus in motion, the ever-streaming sky, night-driven, electric, westward into the city . . . *e lucevan le stelle* . . .

▫   ▫   ▫

At the age of eighteen toward the end of my freshman semester at UC Berkeley, having been plucked by a young man in Boston and kept vibrating on the telephone for five months, sharpening my skills at melodramatic exhortation and blame—cornered as I was in a shared dormitory cubicle casting a stark modernist light on my nineteenth century poses (fainting in a ripped negligee on the forlorn floor of an imaginary boudoir)—I burned up the phone line unassuaged and unexamined, pleading, ignited, exquisitely selfless and thus self-absorbed, tenderized by long-distance, and thoroughly invaded. Fingering the black rotary phone's empty alphabet holes—His name? My name?—I heaved and sank, palpitating like an anemone and laid bare like a shucked mollusk. My bottomless susceptibility encouraged Al to listen while talking little, but his Boston realism brought closure to conversations I hoped to extend. Frustrated to surfeit at last, I leaned into a decision for action: I would go to a gay bar across the Bay in San Francisco and test my . . . errrr . . . testicles.

And so began a journey of a thousand nights and more in these bars, oscillating between exaltation and despair, as I tried to get laid in the name of love and got laid in some other name and walked back into the night to try again, the bars' names—vibrating rhythm—a vatic invocation: Pearl's, The Rendezvous, The Capri, The 524, The Rainbow Cattle Company, The Mind Shaft, The Stud, continuing for decades, sacrificial rite in which my body was meat to placate the hungry/angry god but also the god's own feral pleasure brought to fruition. It's hard to register, now, the charge the mere phrase "gay bar" had then, with its overtones of forbidden treasure and perilous, secret shame, its aura of biblical topos recalling both burning sin and angelic rising, its contradictory tenor fusing the phrase into a single Janus word—"gay-bar"—where one side was leaping in joyous release and the other was locked for eternity in a penitent cell. There was no other community site, no other avenue, no public visibility, no other home away from home.

At my venture out, in December of 1965, the nights were dark and the sex was still (thrillingly?) secret. The gay movement's—not yet a movement—epiphanic libido and horizontal fraternity had not yet come to purpose, though a telepathic reaching toward light was immanent, subject to history's own propulsive network of radical connectivity. You couldn't yet see the combustive, allegorical power in naming your urges out loud to follow them into flame. The circuit through erection and deflation began again each morning or night with impossible innocence and welcome erasure, without yet stringing the stations together—shared bed/empty bed—into a linked strategy of social recognition, petition, and redress. At eighteen I merely gathered myself sobbing or gathered myself thrilled and combed my hair—I will tell you how I combed my hair—and mapped out the even-now antipodal trajectory from Berkeley to San Francisco, coded in the form of the F bus, laconic bullet into the heart of pulsating distance, whose course of freeway to bridge was almost ludicrously symbolic. I paid my fare—the price was admitting I wanted to go—and cast myself into the classic fog in search of reciprocation.

⊡   ⊡   ⊡

My point of view at every point is ineluctably recursive: *Later I would come to see* or *in time I would think that* or

after a few years I started to . . . So many days and nights
collapse into each other, so many hours went in circles,
so many men traded faces, so many dicks went up and
down. My superannuated lenses double, triple, quadru-
ple events. Down a side street, through an alley, across
a corridor, behind an unmarked door: These were
repeated coordinates, and the first of many sets of
indices attaching eros to underground, splitting it off,
Dante-esque, from *la diritta via* to find or lose its only
other way, *in* the night and *of* the night, and cast off into
the castaway arms of the Tenderloin, the emptied financial district, of neon-wicked North Beach. But winding
wide-eyed into these alleys I didn't even know to say
hello and goodbye—a little boy with a hobo sack made
of a polka-dot scarf and a wand—because I couldn't
then see the contraindications of audience, old family
and new family crossing in opposite directions. (Five
months later, already long removed from the machin-
ery of home and former friends, spiraling into new net-
works of bar-goers and bed partners, I walked the
dormitory grounds one spring evening with Lela, old-
est and dearest pal, who turned suddenly to me and
pleaded, "What do you do all those nights you say
you're doing nothing?") Now in the dark, bus-weary but
alive with singular focus, I tucked in my striped shirt
and settled my stomach which had lurched the first of
a thousand or more lurchings; I took off my black

glasses to cast my lot with being seen over seeing. This Tenderloin bar was Pearl's, an after-hours club open to underage explorers. A couple of weeks ago I'd been initiated with my good friend Mark after we'd mutually removed our masks—*girlfriends!*—and formed a scandalous compact of adventure. This time I was on my own. I smiled at the doorman like a practiced pro—a thin, wavering smile, for sure, but bravely set—and swam into the bowl of a room with naive guppy enthusiasm, all goggle eyes and forward momentum.

I emerged into the peopled circumference of a dance space, whose center was occupied by bouncing boys, semi-collegiate or flightier than that, wiggling to the Supremes while the circumference slid around them at a slow, ogling pace. Far in the back, on a stage-like dais, was a civilized set of tables, gents talking to gents, vestigial normalcy. Colored lights fractured and energized both circulating loop and throbbing core, and everything else throbbed, and I throbbed too. I stood at once airy and leaden, predatory and perfectly succulent, putting on my thick, black-rimmed glasses to scan the crowd, then taking them off in case anyone had noticed. I put them on and took them off, put them on and took them off, wading slowly through the periphery, penny loafers leading the way. I was as neat as a cut-out silhouette and about as loose; my Oxford shirt was tucked in all the way to my shoes, and my hair—well, I will tell you about my hair—but I managed to get some depth of perspective by grooving to the music from the outside circle without committing shamelessly to the inner dance.

As I casually pocketed my glasses one more time, a baritone voice from behind me whispered into my ear, "Why not just keep your glasses on?" I turned around; he smiled slyly, swept away in the moving current, leaving me achingly self-conscious but deliciously exposed, caught between sweet blindness and sweet sight. He had a dollop of thick, blond hair—the kind you merely push back with your hand and call it a day—and a stevedore's torso stuffed in a white, cable-knit sweater; he was tall with a fair, freckled complexion and an air of confident athleticism. I started to twitter under the nourishment of his parting eyes.

Time distended as the circling masses looped back. I pretended to be on top of my eyeglass problem (I kept them determinedly off) and did my best to shimmer in the dim light. I hoped that I was being watched, maintaining a passively alert stance, urged toward clairvoyance by my near-blind state, trying to scry a blond fin carving the surface of the crowd. Martha and the Vandellas matched the beat of my knocking knees; I moved my arms like I was dancing in place to mask their tremor, though in truth I was now almost drowsy from stimulation. Then a voice flavored with molasses warmed my ear from behind, enunciating with great, slow, care: "I'd . like . to . fuck . you."

Reader, can you picture me in my starched pinafore, punctured by this impregnating voice? Can you catch my prim shock at the sudden vernacular, my unskilled, flustered propriety; can you feel the pointedness of the remark in that age at my age, before notorious bathhouses, before leather and chains, before public orgies, before AIDS? Beyond that, my entire sexual repertoire was circumscribed by Boston Al's generous rubdown, and he'd even *asked* me with fine politesse if I wanted to try something new before he scooted down to blow me, secretary licking a letter. If I was alarmed and maybe even affronted (What kind of girl did he think I was, etc.) I was also titillated out of my pants. *But I didn't even know his name!*

Such decorousness I communicated without much trouble, given the full extent of my dropped jaw and nervous giggle. The silver shark who'd cruised the room with bloodlit, discriminating intent now bowed low, transformed into a courtier dusting my feet with the florid plume of his hat. Certainly he was sorry, hadn't realized what kind of guy he was dealing with; would I like to take a seat? We removed to the theatrical dais where I tucked up my knees in self-congratulation and began the essential conversation.

Bill, it turned out, was educated, literate, preparing to

get an advanced degree at SF State, with enthusiasms that matched my own: a belief in the lasting value of *Who's Afraid of Virginia Woolf* (my favorite current literary argument!) and a devotion to the Theater of the Absurd in general. From there I was all unstoppable run on:

"I go to Berkeley I'm a poli sci major but I'll probably study English want to be a writer I'm living in the dorms love Ionesco came here once before a couple of happened in Boston for the first but now I'm really ready about love not sex I plan to meet then I'll forever . . ."

Bill nodded ceremoniously, eyebrows raised in approval, laughing as he patted my leg, genially committed to letting me verbalize my entire past and even my future with him. He greeted a couple of passing boys as I fondled my coke, then we talked for an hour about literature and more. Late in the night as Pearl's grew thin, after I was convinced of his genuine interest and had convinced him of my serious purpose, he took me home to his apartment high on a hill above North Beach, precipitous climb to a small modern studio, plate glass and bleached wood, with a wide, rumpled bed almost thrust through the picture window like a gangplank, overlooking the far, glistening, lubricious Bay. And there, gentle reader, without further ado, he turned off the lights and fucked me till the stars were wet with dew.

▣   ▣   ▣

Going to Pearl's was inconvenient at best, given its after-hours schedule (*starting* at 2 A.M.?) and my dependence on the F bus, whose last ride back to the dorms left the East Bay Terminal in down downtown San Francisco a few unaccommodating minutes later at 2:13, not to resume its returning crawl till early rush hour. The real goal would have to be the Rendezvous, cleanest and cruelest of all the collegiate bars, up a long stairway behind a Prohibition-style unmarked door on a quiet, denuded street at the edge of the financial district. For a couple of months I dared an "I'm-with-them/ I'm invisible" slide (being three years under the age limit), and sometimes the bouncers went blind as I nervously held my breath, but soon enough I scored a fake I.D. in dependable radical Berkeley, and my fate was sealed by a hasty wave up to the landing.

The Rendezvous of my near-virginity; the Rendezvous of my counting how many men so far on my fingers; the Rendezvous of sighing across the room while Fontella Bass sang "Rescue Me" and I thought she meant someone else; the Rendezvous of cold, bitter shoulders and men as remote as they were before I said I *wanted* men; the Rendezvous of window dressers imperious in precision slacks; the Rendezvous of the last stand, of being a cute kid, of saying less than I knew so

I could be thought worth doing; the Rendezvous of complete impersonation and lusting after a look of alluring indifference, of purveying a masque of decorum in profile; the Rendezvous: a sweater bar; the Rendezvous of the hunt, and shriven nights, and pointless mornings of long walks to the bus, and somewhere, somewhere buried now because it won't release, moments of wild pleasure and affection in the company of gentle men—but the Rendezvous won't let loose those nights from its faceless, unnamed speakeasy doors I would rip from their hinges, impatient for payback. Nowhere did the prosaic malevolence of the social closet pervade more thoroughly, a mutating force that narrowed men into their slimmest moral territories to fit the imprint of secondhand normalcy—a charade of entropy with a mixed drink—not the multifarious community we would come to be but the constrained, devalued projections into one or two or three tight molds, provisional, good for a quick glance and one moment's respite of being alike instead of different. Cleaned up and smoothed down, brushed off, polished, impeccable, unassailable exteriors.

Today, confirming my history of gay bars in the San Francisco Public Library archives, I happened upon an exhibit of men rounded up and exterminated in Nazi Germany under the aegis of the infamous Paragraph 175—banks of photos of their faces, the sweet fairies of

Germany I hardly needed to examine to recognize, the schoolteacher and artist and writer and yes, the window dresser—so I'm having to remind myself that my own foolishness, my frailty, my comrades' unlovingness, the unmarked doors of their hearts, our unmet Rendezvous, were surrounded by real not imaginary terrors, of police roundups, and lost jobs, and public shame and family disgrace. Last call at the Rendezvous—we stood around drinking, eyeing, and we went home and sometimes talked and sometimes didn't and spread our legs or got spread, we licked and bathed each other in sweat and sometimes traded tender kisses that seemed to matter and sometimes didn't, a repertoire of intimate address played out in a microcosm of distance: the one-night stand, the trick; the Rendezvous which had no warning printed above its legendary unmarked door into which I entered shivering a hundred nights, all in my youth, eighteen, nineteen, not yet part of an army of natural lovers—but I will get there, it will come—not quite yet one of the soldiers of ecstasy.

⊡   ⊡   ⊡

Every night a new night; every wardrobe not yet tested; every shower a purification; each afternoon a systematic prelude. With all the other students gone on movie dates at normal dating hours, the dorms reached a point of (merciful) hushed emptiness as I began my preparations for a 10 P.M. departure to the city. I was slim; I had nice bones and a twinkle above them when I managed to relax, but my hair—oh, my wiry, independent, shtetl hair, my Ukrainian ribbons from my mother's side, folkloric bonnet of curls, was out of the question, way too heavily accented, ruefully unacceptable, untidy, un-Californian, un-Rendezvous. So I stepped out of the shower and looked right and left to make sure I was alone—I was always alone or I wouldn't have begun the process!—and blotted my hair, careful not to rough it up into frizz. I crept back to my room, sat down, took a towel and folded it lengthwise with studious applica-tion—*my* weekly midterm—into an absorbent strip like a civil-war bandage, to heal my wound. Dreamily I thought of clean-cut, uninflected men, exhibiting no scars, no wayward intentions, no minds of their own. I combed my hair down over my brows, wet straight bangs, and wrapped the folded towel across it, knotted behind my head, hair plastered to dry flat on the grid-dle of my forehead. In half an hour, dressed for recov-ery, bandage removed, the vicissitudes of organic growth had been countered by a smooth semi-industrial layer of perfectly straight strands, my fall of grace. Like a sur-geon I pried, parted, and patted. With a comb I lightly pressed and shaped the units—no one would ever know—(later no comb could make it through my afro of sausage curls) into a pompadour-like contraption of near-solid organization, neat, discrete, unshakably—or so I hoped—under control. I unwrapped the telltale, offending towel and put it on the rack. The mirror confirmed my magic from all angles. I flashed a pleased, bitter, triumphant smile, tucked in a loose strand, and hit the door with trembling anticipation, hairdo firmly in place, a swagger enclosing my swish.

⊞   ⊞   ⊞

I got on the F bus to the city. I kept my head down and my hopes high. There weren't many people on the bus that late. A tired woman stepped up with a couple of stuffed shopping bags, looking at me with disgust for the shame inscribed across my face that everyone could see in spite of my near-perfect hair. I kept my head down and my hopes high, as the bus wove on through the ghettos and warehouses of Berkeley, and I traced in my mind the long dark stairway up to the Rendezvous, boys at the top. A drunk sat down across from me, sneering contemptuously at my leaking corruption, my stinking catalogue of projected caresses. I kept my head down with my hopes high, scanning under lowered brow for the towers of the bridge, and beyond them the spangled towers of the city, *fleur de ciel,* the bridge itself a stairway and the city rising. The bus stopped at every lonely outpost of the East Bay, lost workers working too late ascending and descending as the murky waters of the Bay drew nearer. A skinny man with levitating hands I recognized from one of the bars took a seat in the back, sweeping his eyes across mine then lowering them in secret humiliation. I too kept my eyes down but my hopes high, catching the first string of lights on the Bay Bridge, diamond necklace around my trembling throat, as the bus hit the incline, the sour smell of Bay mud drifted up, the bridge unfolded its stairway, the boys of the Rendezvous waiting up there, down there, my skin beginning to itch, my pulse quicken. And there at the crest between the big suspension towers from the top deck heading west the city began to sparkle into view over the salted gray steel, one tall building lit up, another glittering group, a huge gesturing neon sign, the tall silhouettes arced with scintillations, a sense of streaming purpose, one glinting community of buildings with night-vision eyes alive in the dark, glimpsed always through the bars of the sloping cables, an actual *other side*, I drank the elixir of, keeping my head up, now, for clear sight and my abiding hopes rising. A complicity of electricity burned high as I neared the shining metropolis all vicissitudes of school or traffic or psychiatry or family couldn't deny, a shimmer of the western wave exactly at its crest, this fluorescent tournament of arrivals, radiating city at the water's edge unbound.

Even in 1966 I could map its locales as if they were part of my body, and my body recognized the incoming city as a form that fit, though I was too young, I was too small, the city was too big, it had too much to give and I had too much to be taken. If it wasn't yet mine it would become mine. And it *is* always and still this apparitional San Francisco, glistening with the immediate future, starlit, as seen through the scratchy windows of the accelerating F bus from the upper deck of the Bay Bridge as I set out late in the evening to get lost or found—flickering spires between spires—my nose pressed right to the glass in the middle of a night at once pitch-black and luminous I hoped would never end.

▣   ▣   ▣

The East Bay Terminal spilled its contents into the unpeopled nether streets of the financial district, *below* Market Street, it was said, with an emphasis on the *low.* The proverbial canyons were indifferent to my forward-leaning walk except in one respect: Together they polished an unrelenting wind arriving somehow off the Bay, batted it from their right angles to sharpen the chill, and hurled it down Mission Street like a bowling ball of air. The target, of course, was my precious hairdo. I ducked and danced like a prizefighter, keeping my head down and my hands up, a gesture somewhere between vigilance and pained helplessness, fanning my fingers in a frantic attempt at maintenance.

The route to the Rendezvous required navigating only these glaciated throughways. I scampered from entryway to entryway, wedging my body close to the walls, darting out of the aim of sniping gusts, re-plying loose strands as soon as they were grabbed by the teeth of the wind. At a few sacred posts along the way old-fashioned mirrored columns offered their charity. With quick, alarmed focus I assessed the damage, and dexterous as Ariadne trilled my knowing fingers around my head. At the foot of Sutter I held my breath and dashed up the street to the Rendezvous, one hand raised like a bronze shield, turning my face right and left against marauding squalls that tried to lift whole sections from my head in a last-ditch attack. I arrived at the doorway shaken by the volatility of this fifteen-minute walk from transportation to transport, winded almost to tears by frustration and exertion but richly enlivened by the chase.

▣   ▣   ▣

I wasn't special there; it wasn't special that *I* was there; it's what I knew and where I went. I was younger than most, and some looked up to me for that and some looked down; some looked through me, as they often did, and some looked me over—almost, but not quite, as often: inviolable algorithm of gay bars. Sometimes, in fact, I went with Mark or Roosevelt; sometimes I arranged to meet up with Jim and John; but at all times I was there alone, filled with incomprehensible yearning, chattering in the foreground while my eyes fed on strangers in the back. I shuffled my impatient feet, ready to follow them in the trance of a suggested direction like a ouija board: B=L=O=N=D. Sometimes they pointed me out the door with Del or Danny, then trotted me back the next week for Danny or Del.

One blustery night in October I pushed my beginner's luck dangerously through to last call. After a long set of gin and tonics, I heard the bartender's ominous shout, then dared to have one more; I blinked my brown poppy eyes and no one blinked back. Desperate, I tried to prevail on a casual friend for shelter to no effect—sorry, kid—and so, grabbing my coat, with the last scuttling men blending into the shadows like shadows, dashed out the door—2:00 A.M.!—racingly retracing my fraught steps with the now-welcome wind pawing my back, eastbound without a moment to think of lost opportunities and no further second to spare. I arrived at the terminal at 2:15, to breathe in the treacherous fumes of the just-departed last bus to Berkeley, leaving the station empty, chilled, and silent till six the next morning—and where was I now in my hairdo and high hopes?

⊞   ⊞   ⊞

Across from the terminal, at First and Mission, was the
sad castle of my keep: Foster's Cafeteria, open all night
for my unending night, the non-negotiable duration of
despair. One outpost in a Depression-era chain across
the city, it had steam-table food, tank-brewed coffee, and
translucent lime jello; nobody there wanted to be there
because nobody there had anyplace else to go. I ordered
a coffee and sat in a corner with my busted wings in my
lap, as far away as I could from the homeless men and
muttering drunks and street crazies, to differentiate my
predicament from theirs—but only as far as the plate
glass walls would allow, because I was part of their company now, inside the zone of dispossession, undone by
the faulty mechanics of my lust, of even my tender,
untested, zealous love. The gulping loss took my throat
so that I couldn't swallow: no one to be there for me, no
there for me to be, vanished in plain sight under a neon
spray of disinfectant accommodation, some last-chance
saloon of a world-weary cafeteria—but this was my
first chance!

I may have endured one or two such nights again in
the coming months, and each tore down another part of
me, broke me more deeply against the rocks of what my
privilege was designed to protect me from, a middle-class
kid in search of affection within the frame of a polite

dream of possibilities and possession, kicked below the line, thrown away, so that each time I cried in my coffee a little bit harder, cursing the predilection, unchosen, that alone was enough to cancel out my parents' fine stucco house, my good, lucky genes, my college training-in-progress, my dreamy sense of purpose, my benevolent vision. I sat stupefied for hours by the suddenness and thoroughness with which I'd come undone, in a bottomless heartache as hard and sharp as my body could translate into sentient pain, a loss equal to the future of my promised homoerotic heaven for which the dorms had disgorged me in the false triumph of my own determination. I staggered home in the morning drained and somnolent from so much sadness, blinking back frayed visions that were self-accusations that made my condemnation complete: an attenuated spiral of shame.

But by the second or third descent something settled at the bottom of my cup, a small reflective dreg that started to mirror things differently. Perhaps by then I'd already let my sideburns snake half an inch toward my jaw or, just a few months removed from the dorms, swallowed a tab of acid and permitted the trees to carefully show me why. Within the year, I know, I'd met a couple of curiously cast men at the bar: impish Jeremy who played me an LP of Edith Sitwell reciting *Façade* in the pruniest British trill, a high flute of melodious rhyme that still hasn't quieted, and Rasputin-like Jim, who explained wild-eyed in self-transfixing tones how he'd lit up a light bulb in his gripping fist, a mysterious narrative I found perfectly useful to believe. At the outer edge of the student district in my newly rented room I spasmed in psychedelic collapse, then came out the other side with a reading list starting with Plato, a wall-print from the cave at Altamira, and a boxed set of buoyant Bach concerti. Around campus, on an almost weekly basis, demonstrations and student strikes had begun to fracture the university's fictitious calm. It's hard to keep the timeline in focus, its sequence of rapid initiations, inundations, transformations. Some or all of these incidents collected in my cup in the form of a suspended inchoate question or brooding lapse in the sequence of pain, and began to leak into my marooned isolation, as the ache wore down my nerves and I built up a tolerance for the bitter sacrament of cold coffee. If I was tossed out with the partisans of Foster's Cafeteria, perhaps the view from within—from without—had its own compensatory perceptual angle. I might not have put it together in the glare of that brutal aquarium of night, but in my forced truancy of desperate, unsleeping wonder I began to catch a wavelength arriving from another part of the Bay, where, unanticipated and unlooked for by either side, my proximity to the discarded habitués of Foster's Cafeteria began to resemble something more like solidarity.

▣   ▣   ▣

A cathexis of time in space: The foreshortened crush of events in San Francisco 1967/68—the Haight Ashbury, the Summer of Love, the anti-war movement, Janis Joplin and Jimi Hendrix—accelerated maturation, limbs growing from other limbs, personal and civic body politics rumbling, a protean upheaval underneath the streets as ferocious as the fabled earthquakes. I lose the thread by which I can declare intentions my own, subject to a multi-directional and constant stream of cultural invention. In the narrower terms of my vexed romantic exploration, the tide shifted me away from the circumspect, self-loathing Rendezvous, and towards the randier bohemian shores of North Beach, with its post Beatnik libertine glow, its practiced, seamy boulevards, and free-floating literary sheen. On upper Grant Street, just two blocks from the illustrious City Lights Books, the tiny, cramped, smoke-thick Capri became, for a while, the righteous center of my exploration.

I drove over with friends, or for a short while in my own VW bug, or even stood on the freeway ramp at University Avenue and hitched my way across the Bay with careless, confident ease, with the same incandescent fantasy appearing like a promise at the apex of the bridge, and the same leap into my throat of wide-open anticipation. Inside the Capri, at the very back, which is to say the other end of a dark lozenge not big enough to have a back, we danced in a modest frenzy, shook our hair which was just about long enough to shake, nuzzled a neck with a moustache or baby beard, rattled a couple of beads, and semi-furtively passed a joint—the old-fashioned kind that took two stogy missiles to give you a buzz. My own hair was now a wavy nest looped behind my ears, proudly accented by a bandito moustache that conspired to make me look even younger by showing how hard I was trying to look old. But I *was* an adult now—no more fake I.D. for me—and poetry and high lit were steadily invading my conversation, ably handled by the quirky intellectuals frequenting the bar, many of whom made North Beach their home, down Grant Street inside minuscule rooms in a seedy residence hotel that clearly had never seen better days, with the inspired lyrical name of The Bachelor's Quarters, just one short step removed from Tennessee Williams's infamous Tarantula Arms.

But I'm wrong to put a spider web around The Bachelor's Quarters, because it became my sanctified home away from home, in the skinny but well-formed arms of Stephen, in the cramped thick of his tiny room and single bed, under the fall of his long straight hair, his lean, hawkish gaze and critical wit, in a happy grace incomprehensible to him who both lusted after me with relish and wearily tolerated my youth in equal measure. He was twenty-eight to my twenty-one, and treated me like the pleasant pup I couldn't understand I still was. But in that maddening close chamber stuffed with books and sheet music and bigger books again, under the spell of his independence and in conversation with his friends—a writer, a harpsichordist, a gardener, an historian—I began to see a place for myself in a totally queer collective zone I would later come to know as "community."

By the fall of 1968 the air around the Capri was salted with historical imperative, as if a solution had reached its maximum saturation and was ready to be transmuted into another property entirely, atmosphere becoming ground. In and out of the arms of Stephen, and with other men in and out of mine, I (we) turned passionate encounter into play, and body friction into recreation (many years later, someone at the café suggested, "Don't say 'slut,' say 'sexually *generous.*'") In a gathering political synthesis still liminal but impinging, I sensed a common ground with radicalizing elements at large, and though I couldn't yet precisely see the purpose we shared, the flower had already cracked the bud in me and was unfolding.

It was no big deal to test last call at the Capri: In a jam I just held out my thumb on Broadway and a VW van picked me up and took me back across the bridge. Let's say one night in November I stayed too late carousing, and hadn't yet arrived at an acceptable conclusion. Let's say a number of other men were similarly disposed, if not quite sure of their direction. Let's say some of us knew each other and some of us wanted to, and one or another of us *meant* to, and somebody *had* to, and when the bar expelled us into the dimly lit street a reluctance that was an excess of libidinal energy and fleshy good will restrained our feet, and we *didn't* blend into the shadows. Let's say one person put his back to a blue parked car and leaned, scuffing his boots, and then another stopped and talked, and soon a small set of tired but still-alert men milled around in the smoldering dark out in the open as the safe-house of the bar shut down, *in* the nightglow but not *of* the night. With a smile I put my comradely arm around Michael who was *always* flirting, though I had eyes just then for his friend from Modesto. And the still air was sharp and clear and, yes, *e lucevan le stelle*, as we shuffled in place under the dim streetlights chatting towards any destination at all, and our small, friendly gathering was perfectly visible and absolutely audible to anybody wanting to listen or look—for a good twenty minutes right there on a short stretch of Grant street in 1968 in front of the Capri bar in the middle of the vivid dark of the city we came for together—and then the circle relaxed its hold.

I uncurled my toes on a deepening breath, bade a sweet good night to Michael and "Modesto" without regret, ambled a few blocks down Broadway to where the freeway ramp floated off to the Bay, buttoned up my pea coat, and stuck out my thumb.

HUSH

I'm completely taken with the hammock under a huge maple tree in my third annual rented summerhouse (teacher's prerogative) for July's searing blast of California heat—just twelve miles north of the city, but as far from its soppy fog as, per Dickinson, "firmament to fin." The hammock's like an awning of green and white stripes (but it's under you rather than over you); the material is padded sailcloth, wide as a bed (not one of those acrobatic nets) so you're thoroughly supported *and* cushioned as you rock, enveloped in a lullaby of shade.

The leaves of the maple grow close to the limbs on short branches and long stems—the tree must get pruned regularly—and they cluster densely almost like fur, rounded mounds of foliage rich with shadowy hues. There's such a mass in any given section you can clearly see the tree's strategy: Star-shaped leaves strain outward to catch every changing slant of sunlight, their surfaces projected flatly into the air by lengthy stems, little tilting planes of absorption. The whole structure of trunk, limb, branch, stem, and leaf has geodesic integrity, bright-green pentagrams splayed over a wooden frame.

I've sufficient time to contemplate the teleology of

this tree, slung on my back in voluminous shade, arms outstretched like a giant leaf—but angling for the falling shadow, not for light—alone under a dome of dense, green silence. Then I lie on my side, or curl like a kitten, long removed from my stride that pushed this sling into motion, but still gently rocking. It's only my breath, I see now, that swings me over the long grass, the slight, purposeful push of a pulse.

None of this is mine, you know: not the cottage, not the maple, not the yard; not the fat, flouncy, pink zinnias or black, black violets with yellow nose-nubs; not the old, long-limbed California oak next door, yearning across four lots, or the zooming redwood two blocks away, or the hip little town with its quaint, corny streets, or the wind, of course, that deconstructs this shade into droplets, spattering me with afternoon sun.

I could grow old in this hammock; I have grown old. I'm not who I meant to be, but not not. I lean back—boat in the air—barque on its way. School's out for a while, again. I drink thick coffee; eat fat, bruised peaches, sugar-heavy. I read in every position, floating on words. "Vowels that elope with ease," says Keats, "and float along like birds o'er summer seas." The arc of the sun makes no inscription on this unlit zone. I cross my arms in the mummy position and sway.

THE DANCE THAT WE MADE

History has a way of rearranging dots on a graph: Hairpin turns stack decades, and bind seemingly unrelated events; long curves expand in the middle, stretching linked acts into islands. In the end, sequences may melt into simultaneities, or drift apart like clouds forgetting rain. So when Richard asked me, a few years back, to write the text for a dance about AIDS, I had to lower my body into a graph to see what I still felt, to chart what remained beating near to my heart, or what had diminished all the way to echo.

Richard himself was returning to life as a dancer after his lover's death, after several years of his own struggle with HIV, and was making his own daily tests of flexibility and fortitude. Though in the '90s I'd written a book about AIDS, my immediate senses told me it had happened too long ago: I wasn't sure I could still capably represent the immediate peril and collective saturation, the daily loss and daily triumph I'd once felt (even as a "healthy" man) in pandemic-era San Francisco. I was ready to surrender my impulse to collaborate, and as a kind of apologia, began a formal "letter" of explanation, a substitution, a letter dance.

⊞   ⊞   ⊞

Dear Richard,

I hallucinated you in the park today—just a guy-shadow with a similar shape—and for an instant I was able to project myself into you, enter your skin, and for an instant, I saw, possibly speak from there. It took a physical shape to seduce and activate me, where mentality and abstractions had left me wordless. A body knows from which it speaks. A body is full of information. In my thoughts I can sympathize, I can scrutinize, I can inventory and I can pray, I can ask shapely questions, suspend answers, I can even imagine myself toweling off your night sweats or carrying you up four flights of stairs if I had to. My experience resembles these actions. I can't describe your dead lover; I can't be your wounds or heal them; I can't accompany you on your well-earned victory laps. I can't be suitably astonished by the agonized body's driving force to remake itself again and again, though words resemble these experiences. I'm less than a survivor: I've just been living.

⊞   ⊞   ⊞

I'd wanted to offer Richard something in lieu of necessary comprehension, and I knew a "story" that still wanted telling. But to write about friends dying from, surviving, or transcending AIDS, didn't I need to shoulder some burden of history, to acknowledge the frame enveloping the frame? Even now—several years after I began my letter to Richard and eight years since Marshall's death—when I'm unexpectedly seized by the untold narrative, I still wonder whether giving Marshall's death its due requires placing it *inside* the raging epidemic, San Francisco of the '80s and '90s, inside a frame of other frames, a grand, dramatic, panoramic gallery unspeakably long, or just an everyday family album stuffed with helplessly demotic snapshots. Ah, the vital tenor, the pressure, the grief, the accuracy, the lift, the loss, the loss, the names, the language, the infancy, the phantasm, the new old age, the pure volition, the surrender, the schooling, the tender vigil, the words spoken out loud or not spoken at all or murmured into the mystery of the night, the words held in abeyance in a secret pocket for another time, another room, another improvised blessing or curse . . . But a personal request was hanging in the air; at least I might be able to offer Richard a tale to spark his dance. So in place of any newly awakened text I might muster, I continued with the letter.

▣   ▣   ▣

My dead friend Marshall wants me to tell you part of his story, which I observed, and which I have remembered. His final frailty was thorough and precise, a total deconstruction, so complete it remained out of reach of sentimental projection or exaggerated sympathy. His wasted body small to begin with dwindled inward to a point, a disappearing act, a fact. His ears gone deaf three months previously, his eyes shut down to light and shade: a secret man. That might have been his story if you hadn't known the people we've known.

He'd been raving semi-coherently about a lovely man who'd been delivered to him by a friend—the last newcomer to be actually seen (though Marshall had barely known him, and he'd already departed weeks ago)—and who'd become, *since* then, blind Marshall's spirit guide, his angel of death (I thought) to whom he spoke lovingly and reverently as an eternal beloved— pure intimate address—when others were gathered around, and often when they weren't. "Arno," who even in absence kept Marshall's vocabulary elevated with thrilling, seat-of-the-pants passion and courtly, troubadour vows.

Arno, whose lyrical name and recollected visage
Marshall then placed on anyone else in actual
attendance, speaking with fervent, conspiratorial fixation, *"There you are."* We were all guises
of this one demon lover, whose skin and face
slipped over each of us like a sheath, and whose
interactive, high-minded ardor we duly imper-
sonated. We didn't correct Marshall, since in
our friendships we resembled this devotion. We
were all of us willingly *Arno.* A convention of
Great Beloveds assembled in his room or near his
bed, and we each entered the cottage zone pre-
pared for this hushed intensity, the last cleared
circle of theatrical redemption: love in bloom.

▣   ▣   ▣

I put my letter to Richard aside for a while. A story is
not a dance, I knew, but I had in my hands only what
I had in my head. Stories, I know, circle even when
they aren't told (the letter was written but wasn't sent)
so that even now, years later, I'm driven, again, to tell.
On *this* day in April after relentless, record-breaking
rains, the sun—hello, stranger—has yanked up the
first alarming crop of wildflowers, and the word "bouquet" is fresh on my tongue from yesterday's email (I'd
petulantly told a recalcitrant potential date that I had

"collected my little bouquet of 'no's'" and would wait for *him* to contact *me!*). In this floral melodrama, Marshall inescapably sits on my shoulder once more, and I return to a letter never sent and never really completed to finish a narrative looking for continuity.

▣   ▣   ▣

Zalman, Marshall's main caregiver, had given over his bungalow to Marshall's final months, his final days, his breath or two, this winnowing fade. Through the Petaluma summer's long heat, Marshall had tended a small backyard garden, prize endeavor and joyous, creative tether. By August his eyes were gone, but the garden was bright in his heart and he was kept apprised of its progress. Now, at last—September's flourish—the plot was in high bloom. From the blind bed on which his bones floated, Marshall asked Zalman, one of the only friends whose personal touch he actually recognized (one of the few who weren't "Arno"), in a voice part solicitous and part rich with command, "Bring me some flowers, please."

Zalman went to the back of the house and cut a fine bouquet—flowers resemble our best intentions—then happily brought an overflowing

King of Shadows   165

vase to Marshall in bed: buoyant zinnias in tran-

vase to Marshall in bed: buoyant zinnias in tran-
scendental hues, pledge and proof of summer's
forward-looking zeal. He guided Marshall's
bony hands to feel the curl and bend and flute
of each open corolla. With delicate care Marshall
sculpted in air, lightly caressing petal and crown,
molding the blossoms into a proud, pantomime
bouquet. He leaned forward to inhale, where
hearing and sight were beyond him, to bring
into his body this fist of full bloom. A small
shudder rolled across his face. Slowly, carefully,
Marshall grasped the brimming vase in both
hands and thrust it across the wide bed directly
toward Zalman. Then with arms outstretched
and filled with flowers, he whispered excitedly,
"They're for *you!*"

Dear Richard, this is my dance for you, insofar
as it resembles the movement you can make of
it. I've seen such things!—some of which I can
tell, in the small ways in which I'm the sem-
blance of the friends I've known. This world, in
the end, "corresponds to itself," of which we
partake with gusto.

⊞   ⊞   ⊞

The tentative letter remained uncompleted inside of my computer. In the end, I flew from San Francisco to New York in order to watch Richard dance in his studio, to see if his living, gesturing body could awaken in mine the necessary memory of the necessary urgency of AIDS— cast now as the measure of *his* endurance. In a rickety downtown studio, on a folding chair in the filtered light, I felt Richard's muscles pull against their limits, then trembled with the challenge each extension and propulsion made visible. Within minutes his movement *remembered* me, made me actively engaged in a long struggle familiar, estranged, but retained in my body the way steps imprint themselves in a dancer's corporal recall. I proceeded, then, to collaborate with Richard on a new solo for him, while Paula composed a score: text, movement, music in alliance, a model of walking, looking, and thinking. In the piece, Richard's slow-motion weave through space is a paced enactment of composure and focus. Against gravity, amidst the hurrying furies, he has surrendered to the fixity of his own deliberate gaze.

Here is the opening of the dance that we made:

> Sky panels move and shift. Things move *through* them and *in* them. Clouds, birds, airplanes; the spires of tall buildings. The sky moves *in* me and *through* me. Air currents swirl and bend; my back bends forward in the wind.

King of Shadows   167

On the pavement in a gray puddle the sky shimmers bluely, a pinch of white dissolving as the cloud-wisps drift.

Sky panels scroll and shift. The fat, feathery clouds are bunched with gray bottoms, white contours. A sea-blue hole like an eye watches a gull swoop. It moves *under* the sky, not *in* it. A corniced building cuts into the edge of a cloud mass, where a darker gray comprises the heart of the cloud. It moves *in* me, not *over* me.

Sky panels widen. A gleam of sunlight pulls at the feathers of the clouds, spreading them but also spreading the gray—which turns darker, thicker, as if a fuzz were on it. Patterns of shadow cut and lace the pavement, moving *over* it and *on* it. The red in the brick wall pulsates, then fades.

Sky panels shuffle and tense. White serrates the middle of a cloud bank, then rips. It tears *through* me and past me. Car hoods shine metallic under the glare, almost wet with light. A seam of blue widens then closes, sutured. A small hole stays visible, and light rushes into it. It folds shut, but lip edges are flushed with white.

They're absorbed inward and move off. Two pigeons punctuate the rooftop in silhouette, featureless but ruffled against the shifting gray.

A panel of sky unmoving. It holds me and I hold it. Layers and layers of petaled gray, deeper and deeper towards a whitish core, where a wash of light hangs suspended. The interior panels congeal and separate, but the outer frame remains whole, fixed. It sucks *in* and blows *out*. A taxi idles, pulling the sky into its windshield where no passenger sits, as if a streak or a flash were frozen.

Sky panels shift and move. Bright masses push gray masses out of the way, making the outspread wings of the pigeons transparent. A flare of sunlight catches the rooftop, turning the granite metallic. Something like heat falls from the sky, passing *through* me. A gray mass nudges past the white. A woman's hair stands perpendicular in the breeze, pointing toward the sky, which coalesces around a dark spot then disperses. An island of blue is glimpsed *inside* the clouds; it's *behind* them and *through* them; they move *over* it and *on* it, but they don't move past it. The nearest cloud seems to silver the whole street. I move *in* it and *on* it as the sky moves through.

THE IMMEDIATE LOCAL

As an inveterate city dweller who nevertheless craves immediacy in nature, I spend a lot of time in parks. San Francisco is gifted with blooming coastal cliffs; bayside marshes; rugged, glittery beaches. It has the famous long expanses, pools, and glades of Golden Gate Park, with century-old cedars, redwoods, tree-ferns, Monterey pines, but also the small gnarly hill called Buena Vista, whose hereditary mandate to the city is "keep it wild," and on whose pitched hillsides all the local aged trees grow together in profusion, alongside pungent, yellow-bud acacias; splatted clusters of orange poppies; hale, spiky leptospermum in various mauve; and pink or white flowering plums with their bite-size scarlet balls. Squirrels abound in chirpy abandon near green-glinting hummingbirds; crude, black, blatting ravens; vigilant, sky-high hawks, and they scamper blithely past the legs of ever-wandering, libidinous men aroused, too, by the wild, unruly spark that brings this park to continual fruition square yard by square yard.

Today, as is so often the case, February has cracked itself open to reveal a balmy spring morning: warm sun, a few threads of high mist, new long grass as green as it'll ever get, permeated all by the gratefulness such a suspended day in early February brings, with its hungry respite and promise of similar openings soon to come in multiple.

Sensations mark a few coordinates, but you have to stop and fill in the blanks to find "the manifold meaning of every sensuous fact" (Emerson). My dizzied head, brimming with the runoff from occupationist wars, poisonous governance, personal economic fragility, is coming to level in a graced spot of temporary sunny cohesion. Whatever you have distinguishing terms for gets activated by focus, and the matrix of "meaning" flowers, then, inside of "fact," a sustaining implosion. Each concentrated pause opens the charged, interrelating heart of matter. "That's a *fuchsia pendula*," said Jocelyn, inspecting with a gardener's Latinate skill the backyard greenery we were visiting, and so possessing the plant complexly where I lagged behind in barely cognizant fuzziness: just a momentary bush I was brushing.

I reached a point, a while ago, to which age, in part, had delivered me, where I was full of names and their narration—specific event, color, and line—and my senses were eager for fusion. Meaning's halo hovered as lure over each impression newly engaged or fervently re-staged. I discovered an urge to braid in place and remember . . .

This morning I've moved myself—classic day off—from the park to a convivial outdoor café—another act of public surrender, embraced by the clement city and its awakening streams of air. San Francisco, the anti-imperial, is a festival of neighborhoods, and holds you calmly in its cups, hill to valley. Along the café's wooden bench I eavesdrop on Spanish being spoken to my right, secretly stroke one man's prominent neck, gaze at the widening sky. Like others I get flattened by work, riled by the warrior lords, taken apart by desire, but the city's multiple sympathies manage to stand for coherence: It has zones of permission and pockets of fair value that activate sensibility, and a gentle, gathered demeanor which sweetly resembles domestic life. In its crisp but languorous atmosphere (so confusing to New Yorkers who invariably announce, perplexed, "Doesn't anybody work?") you move and breathe a little more slowly— even I who walk leaning into the wind when no wind is driving. As a civic frame it fosters specificity, cool proportion, and the temper to look and listen. It proposes for your delectation the Immediate Local: small particulars brought to dimension by lucid, northern light— cherished, here, as amplitude . . . as immensity.

NOTES

"The Shrine," p. 9, Virginia Woolf, *The Waves* (New York: Harcourt, 1931)

"Reciprocity," p. 21, Denise Levertov, "Annuals," *The Sorrow Dance* (New York: New Directions, 1966)

"Along The Way," p. 26, George Herbert, "Affliction (I)"; Samuel Taylor Coleridge, "The Aeolian Harp"; Percy Bysse Shelley, "Ode to the West Wind"

"Geomancy," p. 33, Arthur Rimbaud, "Le Coeur Volé"

"King of Shadows," p. 35ff, all underlined quotes from William Shakespeare, *A Midsummer Night's Dream*; p. 45, Ernest L. Thayer, "Casey at the Bat"; Henry Wadsworth Longfellow, "Paul Revere's Ride"; Hugh Antoine d'Arcy, "The Face upon the Barroom Floor"; p. 46, Ezra Pound, cited by Robert Duncan, *The H. D. Book*

"Blue in Gray," p. 71, Walt Whitman, "Song of Myself"

"A Discovery," p. 75, William Carlos Williams, "Asphodel, that Greeny Flower," *Pictures from Breughel* (New York: New Directions, 1962); Ralph Waldo Emerson, "The Poet"

"The People's P***k," p. 77ff, *The Letters of Robert Duncan and Denise Levertov* (Stanford: Stanford University Press, 2003) and unpublished corrsespondence; p. 86, Robert Duncan, "A Natural Doctrine," *The Opening of the Field* (New York: New Directions, 1960); p. 90, Robert Duncan, "Circulations of the Song," *Groundwork: Before the War* (New York: New Directions, 1984); Denise Levertov, "The Jacob's Ladder," *The Jacob's Ladder* (New York: New Directions, 1961)

"Dahlias," p. 95, Robert Glück, *Jack the Modernist* (New York: Serpent's Tail, 1988); Aaron Shurin, "July," *Unbound: a Book of AIDS* (Los Angeles: Sun & Moon Press, 1997)

"Reading in Time / Reading in Place," p. 97ff, Marcel Proust, *Rememberance of Things Past* (New York: Random House, 1981)

"Abattoir," p. 112, Karl Soehnlein, *You Can Say You Knew Me When* (New York: Kensington, 2005)

"The Dancers," p. 118ff, Ivan Turgenev, *A Sportsman's Sketches* (New York: Everyman's Library, 1992); p. 119, Walt Whitman, "Song of Myself"

"Avatar," p. 125, Samuel Taylor Coleridge, *Anima Poetae*

"In the Bars of Heaven and Hell," p. 131, Jack Spicer, "The Holy Grail," *The Collected Books of Jack Spicer* (Los Angeles: Black Sparrow Press, 1975); W. Jackson Bate, *John Keats* (Cambridge: Harvard, 1963)

"Hush," p. 157, Emily Dickinson, letter to Higginson, June 7, 1862, *Emily Dickinson: Selected Letters* (Cambridge, Massachusetts / London, England: Harvard University Press, 1985); p. 158, John Keats, "To Charles Cowden Clarke"

"The Dance that We Made," p. 159ff, "Bonus Round," text by Aaron Shurin, music by Paula Kimper, choreography and dance by Richard Daniels

"The Immediate Local," p. 169, Ralph Waldo Emerson, "The Poet"

Grateful acknowledgment is made to the following publishers for their permission to use material:

New Directions Publishing Corp. for "Annuals" (excerpt) by Denise Levertov, from *Poems 1960–1967,* copyright © 1961 by Denise Levertov. Reprinted by permission of New Directions Publishing Corp.

New Directions Publishing Corp. for "The Jacob's Ladder" (excerpt) by Denise Levertov, from *Poems 1960–1967,* copyright © 1961 by Denise Levertov. Reprinted by permission of New Directions Publishing Corp.

New Directions Publishing Corp. for "Ashodel, that Greeney Flower" (excerpt) by William Carlos Williams, from *Collected Poems 1939–1962, Volume II,* copyright © 1944 by William Carlos Williams. Reprinted by permission of New Directions Publishing Corp.

New Directions Publishing Corp. for "The Natural Doctrine" (excerpt) by Robert Duncan, from *The Opening of the Field,* copyright © 1960 by Robert Duncan. Reprinted by permission of New Directions Publishing Corp.

New Directions Publishing Corp. for "Circulations of the Song" (excerpt) by Robert Duncan, from *Ground Work: Before the War,* copyright © 1984 by Robert Duncan. Reprinted by permission of New Directions Publishing Corp.

Stanford University Press for "The People's P***k" by Aaron Shurin, from *Robert Duncan and Denise Levertov: The Poetry of Politics, the Politics of Poetry,* edited by Albert Gelpi and Robert J. Berthoff, copyright © 2006 by the Board of Trustees of the Leland Stanford Jr. University. Reprinted by permission of Stanford University Press.

AARON SHURIN is the author of ten books of poetry and prose, including *Involuntary Lyrics* (Omnidawn, 2005), *The Paradise of Forms: Selected Poems* (Talisman House, 1999), and *Unbound: A Book of AIDS* (Sun & Moon, 1997). His writing has appeared in over twenty-five national and international anthologies, and has been supported by fellowships from the National Endowment for the Arts, the California Arts Council, and the San Francisco Arts Commission. Shurin is Associate Professor and Academic Director of the MFA in Writing Program at the University of San Francisco.